D0201161

CLARINA NICHOLS

Clarina Nichols

Frontier Crusader for Women's Rights

Diane Eickhoff (signature)

Diane Eickhoff

QUINDARO PRESS   KANSAS CITY

Publisher's Cataloging-In-Publication Data
(Prepared by The Donohue Group, Inc.)

Eickhoff, Diane.
Clarina Nichols : frontier crusader for women's rights / Diane Eickhoff.

240 pages : illustrations, maps ; cm

Summary: A biography of the early American newspaper publisher and
feminist, Clarina Howard Nichols. Includes an overview of the first
women's rights movement.
Interest age level: 12 and up.
Includes bibliographical references and index.
ISBN: 978-0-9669258-8-3

1. Nichols, C. I. H., Mrs. 2. Feminists--United States--Biography--
Juvenile literature. 3. Women's rights--United States--History--19th
century--Juvenile literature. 4. Suffragists--United States--Biography--
Juvenile literature. 5. Women social reformers--United States--
Biography--Juvenile literature. 6. Nichols, C. I. H., Mrs. 7. Feminists--
United States--Biography. 8. Women's rights--United
States--History--19th century. I. Title.

HQ1413.N52 E532 2016
305.42092 B   2015958003

Adapted from *Revolutionary Heart: Clarina Nichols and the
Pioneering Crusade for Women's Rights*

Quindaro supports the work of the Wikimedia Foundation
which curated many of the public domain photographs and
illustrations used in this work.

Book design by Aaron Barnhart
Printed in the United States of America
Distributed by Itasca Books, Minneapolis, Minnesota

10 9 8 7 6 5 4 3 2 1

Contents

For Sofia Diane

Introduction

On the morning of July 18, 1868, a train carrying the most famous man in America pulled into the frontier town of Manhattan, Kansas. General Ulysses S. Grant was on board. Three years earlier he had led the Union Army to victory in the Civil War. Now he was running for President. All across the northern United States, people gathered to cheer on their hero. At each stop Grant would step out of his private railroad car and bow to his adoring fans. Then he would retreat into his car, and the train would move on to the next stop on the tour.

As the train pulled slowly into Manhattan, an enthusiastic crowd began chanting, "Grant! Grant! Grant!" The general stepped onto the platform, doffed his hat, and bowed. People were close enough to reach out and touch him, but no one dared approach the larger-than-life Grant. And the general was not the kind of back-slapping, hand-shaking politician who wades into a crowd of supporters.

Just then, a tall, plain-looking woman began making her way through the cheering crowd. With one hand she clutched her long, full skirts. With the other, she parted the crowd. Halfway across she caught the general's eye. He gave her a friendly nod. When she reached Grant, the woman thrust out her hand.

"General," she announced, "as one of the mothers of Kansas, I bid you welcome!"

Before the celebrated war hero could reply, she had another message for him, also from the mothers of Kansas.

"If we could vote," she said, "we would vote for Grant!"

His craggy face broke into a broad smile. "You can electioneer for us," he said, pumping her hand.

"Aye, aye," she said in her unmistakable New England accent. "That we can."

The ice was broken, and the men in the crowd surged forward. Everyone was now eager to shake Grant's hand. When the train started up a few minutes later, it left behind a sea of outstretched hands.

Later, a friend who witnessed this scene came up to the outspoken woman.

"You were acquainted with him in Washington?" he asked. "I thought from the way his face lighted up that you had met before."

Clarina Nichols smiled and shook her head no. This was the first time she had met General Grant. She had merely seen him

When General Ulysses S. Grant (shown here in an 1865 photo) decided to run for president in 1868, he was a celebrated war hero. He was quiet and aloof, but presidential candidates in those days were not expected to make speeches.

being stared at "like an elephant" and decided to put him at ease. While she was at it, she would deliver a good-humored message about woman suffrage, the right to vote. After all, opportunities like this did not come along every day, especially in a state so far away from the centers of power and influence.

Few 19th-century Americans spoke up for women as often as Clarina Nichols did. Her beliefs led her halfway across the country to Kansas. And on that summer day in 1868, they gave her the nerve to approach the man who would become the next President of the United States.

How she would have relished a one-on-one talk with Grant.

He knew that women were not allowed to vote, but he probably gave it little thought. Like most people he accepted the notion of separate "spheres" for men and women. He probably also believed that the God-given role of man was to rule over the so-called weaker sex. The result of this kind of thinking was a system of laws that favored men and discriminated against women in many ways.

Women could not hold public office or serve on juries. Public universities were closed to them. All the higher paying trades and professions shut out females. In cases of divorce, if the husband wanted custody of the children, it was granted. When a husband died without a will, his wife inherited just one-third of his estate; the rest was given to the husband's male relatives. Whatever money a married woman earned through her own hard work did not legally belong to her, but could be spent by her husband in any way he chose. And so on. The list of men's rights, and women's wrongs, was very lengthy in 1868.

For more than 20 years, however, women had been challenging these laws and the thinking behind the laws. These women, and the men who supported them, had formed a movement — the world's first women's rights movement. Few women had meant more to that movement than Clarina Nichols. In person, in public, and in print, Nichols had already devoted half her life to opening minds and breaking down prejudices. Her efforts had helped women gain rights in several states and had brought one state into the national spotlight. And her quest for equal rights did not stop there. When slavery threatened to move into the unsettled territories of the country, she uprooted her family in the East to join the freedom fighters in the West.

Toward the end of her life she was featured in a popular book that profiled the 100 most important women of the 19th century. But then the life and achievements of Clarina Nichols began to slip through the cracks of history. Though she had written thousands of articles for newspapers, she had never kept a diary, and she never wrote a book about her life. Over time her papers were scattered and lost as she moved around the country.

Some of her writings, though, found their way into libraries and museums from Vermont to California. Family members, friends, and historians worked hard to preserve her memory. Gathered together, the remaining pieces of her life — letters, newspaper articles, poems, speeches, drawings, photographs — tell an amazing story. Clarina Nichols was both an unsung hero and one part of an unsung multitude of women who spoke up, acted up, demanded their rights, and changed the world.

Part 1

Growing Up

Vermont Girl

Clarina Irene Howard was born on January 25, 1810, the first of eight children born to Chapin and Birsha Smith Howard. She grew up in West Townshend, a small farming village tucked into the Green Mountains of southern Vermont. If Clarina were alive today, she would still easily recognize the countryside — the bend in the river, the valley, the mountains that wrap themselves around the little town like a giant's protective arm.

Chapin Howard, her father, operated the town's tannery, a business that turned raw animal skins into leather for making shoes and horse harnesses. An ambitious, public-spirited, likable man, Chapin later owned a hotel, served three terms in the state legislature, helped organize and finance a Baptist seminary in

Clarina, age three, probably painted by a traveling portrait artist in 1813.

Townshend, and made a small fortune buying and selling land in territorial Michigan. By the time Clarina Howard was grown, her father was one of the wealthiest men in town. Because he was fair, honest, and didn't put on airs, Chapin Howard was respected by rich and poor alike.

Birsha Smith Howard taught her five daughters how to work hard and keep house. Children as young as two or three were expected to help out wherever they could — gathering wood chips for the fire, scattering feed for the chickens, and rocking the newest baby in its cradle.

At a time when one-third of American babies died before the age of three, all of Clarina's seven brothers and sisters survived into adulthood. This was a strong, healthy, prosperous family.

Though the Howards were rich enough to employ servants, Mrs. Howard made sure her five daughters could keep house without help. Clarina learned to cook and clean, but she also learned how to milk cows and take care of chickens. All this was "women's work," as was churning butter, gardening, canning, and pickling.

Every female was expected to learn the sewing arts, for store-bought clothing was expensive and sewing machines had not yet been invented. Clarina was good with her hands. She learned how to make any type of clothing from dainty bonnets to lacy petticoats. Once, after she repaired a badly torn garment with a bit of ribbon, her mother said proudly: "That is Clarina all over — so ingenious!"

Though she could embroider, crochet, stitch, spin, and weave, what Clarina liked to do best was knit. At the end of the day, during a lull in the conversation, at meetings and lectures and church, she pulled out her needles and put her hands to work. She once confessed to a friend that "I can think so much better to the click of the needles." If she began knitting furiously, it was a sign that she was thinking hard. In later years she would learn how to use knitting to political advantage. Wherever she went, people began to associate the click of the needles with Clarina.

The summer she turned eight, a religious revival swept through West Townshend. Revivals were so common at that time that it was said America was experiencing a "great awakening."

Whenever a powerful preacher came to town, word quickly

spread and crowds gathered. Camp meetings lasted for upwards of a week, with people gathering in the evening to sit on hard benches for hours in front of a blazing fire. It was an exciting time for everyone, including the children. All eyes were on the traveling preacher, his face lit up like the noonday sun. In one hand he held a worn leather Bible. With the other he flipped deftly from one passage of Scripture to the next. The climax of each night was the call for people to come forward, confess their sins, and invite the Lord Jesus Christ into their hearts and lives.

In 1818 Chapin and Birsha Howard answered that call — and so did eight-year-old Clarina. She signed her name right below theirs in the register of the West Townshend Baptist Church, which they joined after their conversion.

The young believer took her religion seriously. She read the Bible through several times and memorized many passages. In later years she would be able to hold her own against any preacher who insisted that the Bible was against women's rights. Clarina would declare that these preachers had gotten it all wrong. She maintained that the Bible's central message was universal love, and she could recite the verses that proved it.

But in her youth, religion was less about love and more about laws. Baptists had a strict code of conduct for their members. They were not allowed to drink alcohol, play musical instruments in church, or dance. Later, Clarina recalled being taught that the devil played the fiddle and "to keep step to its music was the march of death."

If the Howards had a second religion it was thrift. Even though they were well-off, Clarina's parents taught their children to live

Clarina's parents, Chapin and Birsha Howard, could be stern with her. But they also gave her opportunities few girls of her day would have.

simply and waste nothing. Clarina had one dress for winter and one for summer. When the next year arrived, her good dress became her everyday dress, and her everyday dress became a petticoat. After it had outlived its usefulness as an undergarment, the material was cut up and made into quilts and hooked rugs. If there was any usable fabric left over, it was turned into patches and rags. Nothing was wasted. Nothing.

Mrs. Howard claimed that thrift was essential for every successful family. She drilled this philosophy into all her children. But being thrifty and pious did not mean that the Howard household was lacking in fun. Clarina grew up in a small, closely knit town with many cousins and neighbor children besides her own brothers and sisters. In winter they all sledded and skated, went on sleigh rides, and played indoor parlor games. Summer brought picnics, hikes, swimming, running around, and made-up games of all kinds.

Throughout the cooler months the Howard family gathered at the end of the day around their large open hearth, the only source of warmth in the house. Out came the work baskets filled with the family's sewing projects. While Mrs. Howard and the older girls patched and sewed, Mr. Howard and the boys repaired their tools or whittled. The younger children played games or knitted mittens and socks. It was a happy time of day.

Family members took turns reading aloud from the week's newspapers or chapters from a book or Bible. They argued about current events and discussed what they had just read. When central heating came on the scene in later years, Clarina declared that the new invention was the "bane," or death, of family life. Instead of gathering around a cozy fire and talking with one another, members of a family could drift away to their own warm rooms.

As a 10-year-old, Clarina played a trick on her relatives, using the fireplace as an accomplice. One October evening a cousin was spinning a spellbinding ghost story as they all sat around the large hearth. Suddenly there was a loud popping noise, then another. The younger girls ran screaming from the room. They were convinced the spirits were speaking to them through the fire. Clarina burst out laughing and called them back. She explained that the "exploding ghosts" were just acorns she had secretly buried in the embers of the fire, hoping to give everyone a good scare.

Other nights Grandfather Smith entertained the family with stories about his narrow escapes during the Revolutionary War. At the end of each evening's stories he would always say, "Oh, my children, you can't know what your liberty cost." Years later, when she herself was fighting for freedom on the Western frontier, Clarina remembered her grandfather's words. Freedom was not free. Someone always paid for it.

Learning Hard Lessons

Though Mrs. Howard had little education herself, she believed it was important for all her children — her daughters as well as her sons. She knew her oldest daughter was smart as a whip. So when Clarina made a careless error, misspelling the word *cider,* Mrs. Howard spanked her. After that, said Clarina, "I took to learning like a duck to water."

By the time she was 12, her parents knew that they had a budding writer on their hands. For her birthday that year Chapin and Birsha Howard gave Clarina a wooden laptop writing desk — a sign they valued her talent with a pen as much as her skill with a needle. She carried that desk with her for the rest of her life. So many letters would be written on it. So many newspaper articles and editorials would begin their lives on that sturdy oak laptop. She may also have used the desk to take notes on the newspapers she read to keep up with current events.

While it was true that the new country had paid a high price for its liberty, not everyone enjoyed liberty's blessings. A million and a half enslaved Africans toiled in the fields and plantations of the South in 1820, when Clarina was 10. Native Americans were being pushed off their lands and moved west. These disturbing realities rarely intruded on life in small-town Vermont. But there was another group of people suffering because they, too, were denied basic rights under the law. And they could be found everywhere in America, even West Townshend.

These were the poor. Many were people just down on their luck, but most of the town's poorest residents were women who were suffering because of the way society was organized and laws were written. They were the wives of men who drank or gambled away the family's money. They were widows who had no means of support. And they were the wives of men who beat and abused them and their children.

At that time there were no federal or state welfare programs. Individual towns were responsible for helping residents who needed help, but the funds were small. There was never enough money to go around.

Chapin Howard was West Townshend's "poormaster." On specific hours of the week, the most desperate people in town came to him seeking help. Often, though, there was little he could do except listen. The law recognized the husband as the master of the household, the lord of his castle. Once married, wives lost all legal rights. Husbands could beat or abuse their wives, take their earnings, and pursue them if they ran away. Anyone who sheltered a runaway wife could be sued and fined for "loss of personal services." It was a rotten system, and Chapin Howard knew it.

Clarina learned many things from her mother, but she seems to have been closer to her father. When she was a teenager, Chapin invited her to sit in a corner of the room and listen in on his interviews with the poor. Many times he could offer no help to his visitor. If a woman was running from another town, for instance, he could not help her because she was not a local resident. Sometimes Clarina saw a tear slip down her father's cheek as he explained why he could offer no help.

Chapin obviously wanted his daughter to hear these stories. Perhaps he wanted her to know that not everyone was as privileged as she was. Maybe he wanted her to feel empathy for the poor and to help them when she grew up. He could not have known what a powerful, lasting impression these experiences would make on his eldest child.

These sorrowful tales left Clarina confused and angry. She could not understand how the law could be used to avoid helping people in great need. Later, she recalled that "I learned to despise such laws and ... doubt the wisdom of the men who could make them."

She concluded that the politicians who made the laws and the lawyers and judges who enforced them did not care. Women in distress, orphans, abused and abandoned women — all these lived in the shadow of the new booming democracy.

Listening to these women was a life-changing experience

for Clarina. She vowed that when she got older she would help women like this. She didn't know how she would do it, but she knew that in some way she would devote her life to justice for these women. Anything less, she said, and "I would shrink from myself as less than human."

When she was 17, Clarina enrolled at Timothy Cressy's Select School in West Townshend. Beyond district (elementary) school, this was her only year of advanced study. It was more education than the average person, male or female, received in 1827.

The following November, the students held a public assembly to show the community what they had learned during their year of study.

The opening address was delivered entirely in Latin. Other "gentlemen" gave talks on mathematics, business, politics, and the pressing social issues of the day, like slavery and the fate of the American Indians. An all-male cast presented two Biblical dramas, including one based on the story of Daniel in the lion's den. A much smaller number of the "misses" gave presentations. Their topics were self-improvement, maintaining good reputations, and looking forward to the joys of Heaven. Others warned the audience of the dangers of spreading gossip, dancing, or — especially scandalous — reading novels.

The one exception to this chorus of distressed damsels was Clarina Howard. Her speech was titled "Comparative of a Scientific and an Ornamental Education to Females." The text of the talk has been lost. What she said can be gleaned from the title.

Clarina Howard as a teenager, in a painting from 1826.

Educators of that day agreed that females from well-to-do families needed some form of education beyond primary school. They called this type of education "ornamental," and it's easy to see why. An ornamental education included classes in poetry, piano, art, fine needlework, singing, and learning enough French phrases to sound refined. Proper etiquette and manners were part of the curriculum. The goal of an ornamental education was to turn girls into ladies with improved prospects for marriage.

A "scientific" education, on the other hand, included classes in mathematics, history, English, Latin, Greek, rhetoric, philosophy, and of course science. Its goal was to prepare young men for the university. The notion that young women should also be offered a scientific education was controversial. That is probably why Clarina wanted to talk about it.

Headmaster Timothy Cressy seems to have taught students of both sexes the same academic curriculum. Probably, though, he did not expect much from his female scholars. Most educators of that time believed girls could not master scientific subjects. Indeed, attempting to do so might actually cause physical harm. After all, girls' heads were smaller than boys' heads. Their smaller brains, people assumed, would have to work harder than boys' brains in trying to master the same material. Teaching girls subjects like advanced mathematics, it was thought, might even endanger their chances to bear healthy children.

At any rate, a scientific education was of little use to a female living in America in 1828. Not a single public university in the country admitted women. A bright young girl like Clarina would not be continuing her education after district school. She would be getting married instead.

All of this may have been on Clarina's mind as she stepped to the podium to present her paper on scientific versus ornamental education. What she remembered later about that day, however, was feeling nervous and uncomfortable. She worried — as she often did — that people were more interested in her looks than in her words. She was striking in her own way: tall, with a long face, high forehead, prominent nose, and wide, full lips. She had a deep dimple in the cleft of her chin, and a steady gaze through intelligent blue-gray eyes. But when Clarina Howard looked in the mirror, all she saw was a skinny, homely girl.

Despite insecurity about her looks, she could project confidence once she started talking. In a portrait painted around the time of her graduation, she looks serious and focused. It is not difficult to imagine her coming to life before an audience. But beneath the surface, the calm young woman staring out from this portrait was burning with ambition and a deep desire to do something with her life.

Clarina's cousin, Alphonso Taft, was in the same class at the Cressy School. Though his family was poorer than the Howards, there was no question that he would continue his education. After completing his studies at Yale, Alphonso would become a lawyer and then a career diplomat in President Grant's administration. His son, William Howard Taft, would go even further. He would become president of the United States and chief justice of the United States Supreme Court.

But at age 18, Clarina was done with her education. Whatever she thought about her cousin going off to Yale, she kept to herself. She had already begun to face a hard truth. It didn't matter how clever she was or how hard she worked. The United States was a land of opportunity for white men.

People of that day talked about separate "spheres" for men and women. The public world was men's natural sphere. The home front was women's. For a young unmarried woman like Clarina, finding a husband was top priority. Together as man and wife, they would take their rightful places in the world. In the meantime, she could teach school. This was an acceptable career for women because it involved the care of children.

"I had a longing desire to do good," Clarina said, "but the teacher's desk was the only sphere that opened before me."

A Promising Marriage

Most of Clarina's friends were thinking of marriage. Some were already engaged. Their spare hours were filled with hemming sheets, embroidering pillow cases, and making other preparations for their special day.

Clarina was not especially looking forward to that day. But what choice did she have? Everything in her world was pushing her to take the first good prospect that came along.

That turned out to be Justin Carpenter.

He, too, came from a well-established, devout Baptist family that had grown up nearby. The couple married soon after they met, in 1830. She was 20 and he was 30. Justin had finished law school, but he was uncertain what to do next. The one thing he

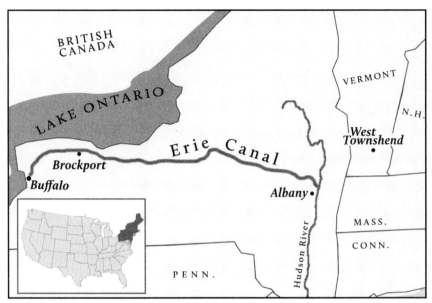

The trip from West Townshend to Brockport was over 300 miles. The first 75 miles overland were the hardest.

knew was that he did not want to stay in small-town Vermont any longer. This no doubt suited Clarina, a reader and thinker who had long been wondering what life was like on the other side of the Green Mountains.

Many Vermonters were moving west at this time. In 1830 the most popular destination was western New York state, along the newly-built Erie Canal. Instead of a long, dusty, jarring trip by stagecoach, Clarina and Justin could climb aboard a comfortable, smooth-gliding packet boat pulled by horses or mules walking alongside the canal at four miles an hour.

Their 300-mile journey ended in Brockport, New York, where they quickly found a home and eagerly put down roots. They needed to, since the Carpenters were already expecting. On March 8, 1831, Clarina gave birth to their first child, a little girl. They named the baby Birsha, after Clarina's mother.

Like many frontier towns in America, Brockport had a superiority complex. Those who had staked a claim along the canal believed that they and their neighbors simply had more ambition, drive, and "push" than those who stayed behind in their Eastern villages.

Justin and his new business partner, J. M. Davis, definitely had "push." They set up a lending library for the town. They started a private school, the Brockport Academy. And Clarina, not surprisingly, became one of the instructors at the new school. She also launched a literary magazine in whose pages she published articles and poetry written by members of the community. She probably also wrote for the magazine, though it is impossible to tell since most of the pieces were unsigned by their authors.

In no time at all this bright young couple had used their impressive talents to move into the center of Brockport society. Perhaps the most important move they made was joining the brand-new Brockport Temperance Society, where men and women would work together for the abolition of "ardent spirits," or alcoholic beverages.

Temperance societies began spreading like wildfire across America in the 1820s, as many citizens became alarmed and disgusted by the rampant abuse of alcohol around them. This was a time when ale, beer, and hard cider flowed as freely as water through the daily lives of most people — including children. People on average drank three times as much liquor as they do today. As Baptists, Justin and Clarina had sworn off alcohol long ago. As a child in her father's office, Clarina had seen how alcoholism destroyed families. She was convinced that if she could save one man from the bottle, she could save a whole family from poverty and misery.

Without hesitation, both Carpenters signed the pledge that sealed their entry into the Brockport Temperance Society. A sample temperance pledge of that time read, "I promise not to drink alcohol in any form for the rest of my life except for medicinal purposes." Within one year of its founding, 400 sober souls had signed the pledge. But even that many temperance advocates were not enough to close down all of Brockport's many grog shops. Instead, the new society would rely on persuasion, using every opportunity to show families of drinkers that there was a better way.

One such opportunity presented itself every Fourth of July. The nation's birthday had been an excuse for a daylong drinking party for as long as anyone could remember. For those who wanted to have their liquor and eat it too, there were Independence Day cakes — huge concoctions that featured a quart each of wine and brandy. Thus soaked to the gills with "good old democratic whisky," these patriots spent the rest of the day shooting pistols into the air, getting into fistfights, blacking out, and falling into the gutter.

To counter this, the Brockport Temperance Society came up with a party of its own: the Cold Water Celebration. Justin, who

Opened in 1825, the Erie Canal used packet boats pulled by teams of mules or horses, as shown in this modern painting, to transport people and cargo between the Hudson River and the Great Lakes.

had been elected one of the society's four directors, dove into the planning of the event.

Early on the morning of July 4, 1831, the men of the temperance society donned their best suits and lined up in front of Wales' Coffee House in downtown Brockport. The women of the temperance society — shining images of purity in their snow-white dresses — lined up behind the men. Next came the town officials, who were happy to support these models of good behavior. Bringing up the rear was an uneven line of wizened old men, many of them veterans of the Revolutionary War, hobbling but in good spirits. Everyone cheered when the old soldiers came into view.

A band playing patriotic music accompanied this parade of Brockport's finest citizens as it marched up Main Street to the Presbyterian Church. They sang, prayed, and listened to long speeches under large, open-air tents. Someone recited the Declaration of Independence. An account in the new *Brockport Free Press*, a pro-temperance newspaper, reported that dinner was served "with coffee, tea, and pure, cold water." It was, the editor of the newspaper declared, "the most pleasing and heart-cheering commemoration of our National Independence that we ever participated in, or ever witnessed."

It was also the high point of the marriage between Justin and Clarina Carpenter. Things were about to go a little crazy.

New York Trials

First there was the notice in the local newspaper. Justin's partnership with J. M. Davis was ending "by mutual consent." Then the Brockport Academy failed. Then the literary journal and newspaper ran out of money and ceased publication. Perhaps strangest of all was this: Justin Carpenter, a law-school graduate living in a thriving boom town on the Erie Canal, was unable to get his law practice going in Brockport.

The young temperance leader was struggling to make his way in the world. And his lack of success was affecting his marriage. Clarina needed him to support her and their baby Birsha. That was his role, his "sphere." But he could not do it. And as the months passed and the money dried up, the situation inside the

This 1837 cartoon shows a well-dressed family that has fallen on hard times during the economic "panic" of that year.

Carpenter home grew increasingly desperate.

There was no marriage counseling in the 1830s, and Clarina was hundreds of miles from any family members who could provide support. She was on her own.

As a child she had sat with her father listening to women in troubled marriages. She remembered the agony in each woman's voice as she begged for money from the village's relief fund. She could not forget the look of despair in each woman's eyes as she was told the village would be unable to help.

Now, when she looked at herself in the mirror, Clarina Carpenter saw that woman.

It would be 25 years before she could put pen to paper and relate the details of her painful ordeal. Even then, she had to write as though it had happened to another woman.

"Her recreant husband failed to provide [and was] too resolute and independent to ask or receive aid from friends," she wrote in 1860. By then Clarina was an accomplished journalist who enjoyed writing with educated words. "Recreant" was just another word for cowardly.

Faced with Justin's refusal to help, Clarina wrote, "she resolved to support the family with her own labor. *And she did it.*"

From that point on, she supported her growing family largely from her own earnings. She took in sewing and boarders, anything for a little cash.

To her guests, she pretended that her husband was the gainfully employed man of the house, and she his "intelligent mistress," fully occupied with her domestic duties. Anyone who was paying attention, however, would have seen the piles of unfinished needlework — far more than any single family could use.

Her new role as the breadwinner infuriated Justin. He had been raised to believe that work was the man's sphere. Even before Birsha was born, he didn't like seeing Clarina go off to work. Once when she was teaching at a female boarding school, Justin raised a ruckus, and soon she was back home again. Now she had the upper hand, and he knew it.

By 1834 the Carpenters had left Brockport — "this scene of past sorrows," as Clarina called it in a letter to her parents. They moved to New York City, where Justin could get a fresh start amidst the thousands of immigrants pouring in from Germany and Ireland. He finally hung out a shingle as a lawyer. He started another publishing company. The couple had their second child, Chapin Howard, named for Clarina's father.

Having another mouth to feed only strengthened Clarina's resolve to never again rely on Justin. She learned of a hatmaker who was looking for women that could do French crimping work at home. This technique for hand-sewing tiny rows of decorative stitches was for expert needleworkers only. Because she was a woman, she was only paid a few pennies per bonnet. Even sewing as quickly as she did, she earned an hourly wage that was far below what a man doing factory work would have been paid.

As miserable as her own situation at home was becoming, Clarina knew that it could be much, much worse. In those days a man had absolute authority over both his children and his wife. He could discipline them in any way he saw fit.

Domestic violence was an enormous problem in early America, in large part because it was widely tolerated. There were no laws against it, and some people even claimed that Biblical law was in favor of it. "Wives, obey your husbands" was a Scripture taken very seriously inside American homes. One Christian minister even claimed that he beat his wife every week with a horse whip, just to remind her who was the boss.

And when a husband abused his wife in public, few people thought of interfering. This was the situation on one of Clarina's trips up the Erie Canal, one she remembered for the rest of her life.

"I saw a middle-aged, stalwart [powerful] Methodist clergyman spanking with his brawny hand a two-month-old baby," she recalled. "Every time the baby cried, he spanked it."

At the same time he was beating the child, the minister was scolding his wife for not following the strict feeding schedule that he had set up for the baby.

Other passengers on the boat looked away, but Clarina could not. She watched the mother, tears rolling down her face, pleading with her husband to stop hitting the child.

"I have less nourishment for the baby than I had at home, and it cries with hunger!" she told him, but to no avail.

A female passenger next to Clarina was watching the spectacle as well. The two women decided that speaking up was more important than good manners. They approached the clergyman.

Your baby is too young to understand discipline, they told him. *You're going to injure your child!*

The minister stopped hitting the baby and turned angrily toward the women.

You have no right to interfere! he snarled at Clarina. *A father has the God-given right to discipline his family in any way he sees fit.*

The two ladies returned to their seats.

Clarina knew full well that this angry, abusive clergyman was correct. The weight of the law was entirely on the father's side. Divorce was rare in 1830s America, and when it did happen, it went badly for the woman. If the father demanded custody of the children, the judge would usually award it to him. And divorce carried a heavy social stigma for women — but not for men. Those were two good reasons for most women not to seek divorces.

Back at the Carpenter home, Clarina and Justin had a third

child together, Aurelius Ormando, named for two of his mother's brothers. She called him "Relie." He was such a happy baby, she recalled, "a treasure sent to check grief's hidden tide."

Neither boy was named for his father. Perhaps Clarina knew, even then, that her marriage was ending and did not want her sons named after their difficult father.

The couple was beginning to drift apart. Divorce would not have been on Clarina's mind at all. Instead, she took the children on extended visits to Vermont, often leaving them with her parents — instead of with Justin — as she went in search of work. She received an offer to return to western New York and start an academy for girls.

As soon as she arrived, however, the whole region fell victim to one of the most severe economic downturns in U.S. history. It was called the "Panic of 1837." One by one, the families came to the school and picked up their girls. The academy was forced to close. Clarina returned to her parents' home.

Meanwhile, back in the city Justin was having more bad luck. Fire raced through the building where he kept his offices and publishing house. There were rumors of arson.

At the college that Justin had attended, a short but tragic note was added to his alumni record: "Burned out and lost all."

Years later, when they were in the women's rights movement together, Susan B. Anthony asked Clarina what the problem had been with her first husband. Was it alcohol? Though he was a leader in the temperance society, he could have been a secret drinker.

No, said Clarina, Justin was as sober as a post. But, she added, she had known many women who were married to alcoholics, and she knew what they faced every day: "defeated purposes, one-sided love, and no support." That was life with Justin.

And it might have gone on much longer, except that one day, for whatever reason, Justin's resentments finally boiled over, and what Clarina called his "malevolent desire to wound" got the best of him. Without explanation, he simply packed up their three children ... and disappeared.

Now she was frantic. She had to get her children back. So she did something she had never done before — she reached out to Justin's family and begged them to help her recover the children.

To her relief, her father-in-law immediately came to her aid. So did Justin's brother, a Baptist minister. They helped Clarina track down Justin and demand that he hand over the children. She took them and left her husband for good.

All of this upheaval deeply affected Birsha, the oldest child, especially her mother's long absences from home. Clarina tried to stay in touch by writing letters. But when her parents read the letters to the children, Birsha would start to cry.

In these letters Clarina included poems written especially for her children. This one, in which she addresses each of them by name, was to be read at bedtime:

> *Aurelius, my son, when day is done*
> *And the moon is up in the sky so high*
> *When the shining stars like laughing eyes*
> *Are hung around in the deep blue sky*

Go look on the moon as the clouds sweep by
And look at the stars that gem the sky
The eye of your mother shall turn to them too
And she'll think of Howard and Birsha and you
And send from far
Through the evening star
On a ray of light, a fond "good night"
"Good Night."
Then send to me through the gentle moon
A sweet, sweet kiss
And I'll see you soon.
Ah, soon!

Clarina filled a thick notebook with her poems. Some were composed on the occasion of loved one's birthdays or anniversaries. Some were for adult eyes only, with themes of lost love, rejection, grief and sorrow: *I cannot love another … Why do I weep? … Days of Sorrow! Nights of Anguish!*

Clarina would not allow herself to indulge in self-pity over her situation for long. In poem after poem, joy followed sorrow as day follows night. Often she would write about the importance of carrying on, even when all hope seemed lost.

Writing was a way for Clarina to stay focused on her future. But it was more than that. Writing *was* her future.

Finding George

By 1840 the shining star of one of West Townshend's most prominent families had returned. There is no sign that Justin stayed in touch with his children or tried to win back his estranged wife. Clarina moved back into her parents' spacious home in West Townshend. She joined the local church and sent her children to school. And while she described herself to a friend as "a wounded dove," she was actually relieved at not having to worry any longer about Justin or their marriage.

By the age of 30 she had rubbed shoulders with immigrants on the streets of New York City, traveled the Erie Canal back and forth many times, and been active in the temperance movement. Though she may not have been fully aware of what was happening, Clarina was slowly being pulled toward new ways of thinking. Back home, she and her father talked about the reform spirit that was cutting through the crisp New England air. Like many forward-looking Christians of his time, Chapin Howard believed everyone was responsible for making the world a better place. What that world should look like was a question that gave rise to newspapers, journals, meetings, and political organizing. The family kept up its steady diet of reading and absorbed many of the day's new ideas.

It did not take long for Clarina to notice that these newspapers were printing articles, poetry, and stories written by women. This was a new development. Mostly they were on matters of home, garden, and kitchen — woman's sphere — but many newspapers also featured poetry written by women, often appearing at the top of page one.

Clarina guessed, correctly, that other stories that were anonymous or signed with an author's initials were also written by women. The idea of having her work published in a newspaper appealed greatly to Clarina. So did the idea of not having her name appear in print. Any notoriety might call attention to her marital troubles and make her children the object of hurtful comments at school or around town.

She began to send her poems and other writings to the newspapers in Brattleboro, some 20 miles away. This was a nice safe distance for a woman who valued her privacy. One of the newspapers was the *Windham County Democrat*, published once a week in a building that still stands today. Its editor was George Washington Nichols, a shy, intelligent, progressive-minded widower.

Outspoken women did not bother him. He had been married to one, and they had raised six daughters. Three of them followed their father into the printing business, which had a tradition of employing women as press operators.

At first, Clarina chose to write on safe subjects, like those her female classmates had chosen for their high school graduation program. And she submitted lots of poems. George Nichols happily published her works, and corresponded often with his young writer. Their letters were friendly, then got friendlier, and then became personal.

They edged forward with their relationship. Each one had questions. Was he looking for a young beauty? She was afraid that when he finally laid eyes on her, he would be disappointed because she was such a "plain person." George, for his part, wondered if Clarina would find an older man acceptable. After all, he was old enough to be her father. She answered that one by declaring that age did not matter to her — she had learned through hard experience that character was what counted.

George replied that he felt the same way. "A jewelry box is not valued for itself, but for the jewels it enfolds," he wrote.

That won her heart.

Clarina was the first to raise the subject of marriage. She could tell that George was a good man — kind, dependable, and forward-thinking. He found her to be witty, intelligent, and sincere. They were a match.

Before she could marry George Nichols, however, Clarina had to formally end her marriage to Justin. On February 16, 1843, the Vermont Supreme Court granted her a divorce on the basis of "cruelty, unkindness, and intolerable severity." Justin's father and brother testified on her behalf. They would stay in touch with Clarina, and that was probably how she learned her ex-husband's fate several years later. Justin Carpenter died in New York City after contracting typhus. The disease was widespread in the 19th century, especially in the overcrowded tenements of large cities. Justin, it seemed, had never found his way in life.

Three weeks after the divorce, an elegant, silver-haired gentleman with dark, bushy eyebrows appeared in the parlor of Chapin and Birsha Howard's home. Taking the curly-haired bride's hand in his, they became husband and wife. George and Clarina had conducted their entire courtship by mail. The double dose of news regarding Clarina's divorce and remarriage took the whole town by surprise. But this was exactly how she wanted it. Her children would have suffered taunts from classmates who found out their mother was divorced — but by the time they did, she was already married again.

Clarina resettled to Brattleboro and her new life in the Nichols household. It was a happy union, and Clarina's children finally had a loving father. Though he was not wealthy, George Nichols was well established as the editor and publisher of a political newspaper. Clarina Nichols set about learning her husband's business. New opportunities were in the air. She was getting a second chance at life and would soon embark upon a career she could scarcely have imagined.

The newspaper business also introduced Clarina to a new set

of friends and acquaintances. Over the years many of them would learn that she had been married once before. Since divorce was uncommon in those days, they simply assumed Clarina had been a widow before meeting the widower Nichols. She never corrected them.

Inventing Deborah

L ocated in the southeastern corner of Vermont, Brattleboro was (and still is) a picturesque town of neat cottages and grand homes. Its residents were community-spirited folks who seemed to go from one meeting to the next. There was a Shade Tree Association for promoting parks, a Thief-Detecting Society for fighting crime, a Brattleboro Book Club, and on and on.

Brattleboro was a town on the rise, thanks in large part to the establishment in 1845 of the Hydropathic Institution, or as it was more popularly known, the "water-cure." This system of ice-cold baths, stimulating massage, simple meals, and pleasant walks through manicured gardens — all under the watchful eye of Dr. Robert Wesselhoeft — promised to heal everything from headaches to kidney problems. It was widely promoted to people with money and ailments that the medicine of that time could not treat.

Visitors began flocking to Brattleboro to stay at the water-cure. Clarina could look out the window from George's office at the *Windham County Democrat* and see a steady stream of stage-coaches. They were arriving with passengers from every corner of New England. When the hotels filled up, families like the Nicholses opened up their houses to out-of-town visitors. And that was how, one summer, they played host to the Longfellows. Famed poet Henry Wadsworth Longfellow visited along with his wife Frances. She had stirred up debate by becoming one of the first women in the United States to use anesthesia in childbirth. (The objections came from clergymen. They claimed women must suffer in childbirth because of Eve's sin in the Garden of Eden.)

Frances Longfellow must have had a lively discussion with Clarina, who shared her interest in health, diet, and natural remedies. Like other progressive people of that time, Clarina had become a vegetarian. She reported feeling better than she had in years. Much of her vigor, though, was probably not due to her new diet. The backaches and headaches she'd had while married to Justin had vanished. She was beginning to see a road that she could travel on. And she was pregnant again.

George Bainbridge Nichols was born February 17, 1844. By this time Clarina's children from her first marriage were ages 8, 10, and 12. With two of George's daughters still living at home, the house was full of family and love.

Shortly after George was born, however, his father developed a

George Bainbridge
Nichols and his father,
George Washington
Nichols, about 1845.

chronic lung condition that not even the water-cure could help. He soon lost the stamina to climb the stairs to the *Democrat*'s second-story offices, to say nothing of performing the many physical tasks required to keep a newspaper and printing business going. His daughters were trained as printers, not writers. If the *Democrat* was going to continue, George needed a new partner in business — so he turned to his new partner in life.

And for the first time, misfortune opened rather than closed the door of opportunity for Clarina.

Most newspapers of that time promoted the causes of a political party in exchange for financial support from the party faithful. When a reader picked up a copy of the *Democrat*, he knew what to expect: news and opinion about the Democratic Party, attacks on the opposition, and lots of reading material that had nothing to do with politics.

At first, Clarina wrote stories for the *Democrat* that were meant to be read by ladies like herself. But then, in 1846, the Democratic Party began to tear in half over the issue of slavery. Clarina began lobbying George to let her put the *Democrat* on record against the expansion of slavery, even though many Democrats were in favor of it. Coming out against slavery might cost the paper the backing of many of its supporters, but George supported her decision.

It was the custom for editors to exchange newspapers with each other. This was how stories and poems from other papers found their way into the pages of the *Democrat*. As part of her education in learning George's business, Clarina kept stacks of newspapers in her parlor. She read them until late in the night by the light of her oil-burning lamp. She took in new ideas as if she were breathing in fresh air at seaside.

She wanted to write more political pieces. But Clarina thought it would help the *Democrat* sell more papers if it had a political voice that female readers could relate to. She still wasn't ready to sign her own name to stories in the *Democrat*. Newspapering was a man's profession. Writing in her own name would bring ridicule and insults raining down on her and George. She didn't know if she could handle that.

So instead, she invented a female character, a salty old Vermonter named Deborah Van Winkle. Then Clarina wrote articles in which she pretended to be Mrs. Van Winkle. She wasn't very ladylike. She spoke her mind. She was everything Clarina wasn't.

In one article, Mrs. Van Winkle went to Washington, D.C., and observed Congress at work. "They tell about women being great talkers," she reported, "but dear me ... I never did see such a strife of tongues! Why, they put a man in the chair to keep 'em in order and to say who shall talk, and what is in order, and what is in disorder, and ... they call him *Mr. Speaker*, jest as if he did the chief of the talking, when he's the stillest and best behaved man among 'em."

By using a little of this country humor, Clarina Nichols, or rather Mrs. Van Winkle, was able to take pointed jabs in the *Democrat* at anyone she pleased — even Democrats. She was speaking up in a forceful new way. Soon she would discover that she was part of a growing community of women who were finding their voices, both as individuals and as part of a movement that was about to change the world.

Part 2

Birth of a Movement

Seneca Falls

Nothing like it had happened before. In 1839, the leaders of the Society for the Abolition of the Slave Trade called for a World Anti-Slavery Convention. It was to be held in June, 1840, in London, England. The Society was a distinguished group of Quakers and reformers who had toiled for decades trying to convince members of British Parliament that slavery had to go — not for economic or political reasons, but because it was morally wrong. Their efforts paid off. Parliament ended the slave trade in 1807 and abolished slavery in 1834, freeing some 800,000 enslaved people across the British Empire.

Now the Society wanted to end slavery everywhere. Its members had their eyes on one country in particular: the United States.

So when notice of the World Anti-Slavery Convention arrived from across the Atlantic Ocean, leaders of the American abolition movement excitedly made plans to attend.

There was, however, one small fly in the ointment. William Lloyd Garrison — publisher of *The Liberator* and the best-known foe of slavery in the U.S. — noticed that invitations to the meeting were only sent to men. Furthermore, it appeared that only men would be allowed to participate in the World Anti-Slavery Convention.

Weren't women half the world?

Some of Garrison's staunchest allies were women. Elizabeth Cady and her fiancé, Henry Stanton, had met in the temperance and abolition movements. They thought it an outstanding idea if they were to marry, attend the convention together as delegates, then honeymoon in Europe.

Lucretia Mott, a prominent Quaker minister living in Philadelphia, helped start the American Anti-Slavery Society as well as the Philadelphia Female Anti-Slavery Society, which was open to both black and white members. One anti-slavery convention in 1838 sparked a riot. Mott and other women had to link arms to safely exit the hall where they were gathered as an angry mob set the place on fire.

These women were going to be excluded from the World Anti-Slavery Convention? Yes, they were! Word came back in early 1840 from England, confirming that only gentlemen would be admitted as delegates at the meeting. But Lucretia Mott and Elizabeth Cady Stanton were not going to take no for an answer. They packed their bags and bought their ship tickets and prepared for

Artist's rendition of the 1840 World Anti-Slavery Convention in London. Note the gallery way in the back, behind a divider. The women shown in the front were the non-voting wives of delegates.

a showdown in London.

When the American delegation arrived at the meeting hall, their hosts stood firm: Women were not allowed to vote or participate in the convention proceedings. However, they were most certainly welcome to sit in the galleries behind a heavy black fabric divider.

William Lloyd Garrison was so furious that he spent the entire convention seated in the women's section.

For Mott and Stanton, the World Anti-Slavery Convention of 1840 was a humiliating experience they would not soon forget. Their shared ordeal forged a strong bond between them, even though they were as different as two women could be: Mott, the older, plain-dressing preacher and Stanton, the young woman with a flair for both fashion and language, who had the words "promise to obey" struck from her wedding vows with Henry.

The World Anti-Slavery Convention proved to be historic, all right, but not for the reasons that its organizers had intended. Their indifference to the women, and the anger they sparked in Elizabeth Cady Stanton and Lucretia Mott, led directly to the world's first women's rights convention.

It was the summer of 1848, and the Stantons were living in up-state New York, near Mott's sister Martha Wright, also a Quaker abolitionist. Mott was paying a visit, and Elizabeth soon joined the gathering. Over the years the two had talked about holding a convention devoted entirely to discussing women's rights. Now, with Martha and other women present, the idea finally began to take shape.

They decided to hold the meeting in one month at the Wesleyan Methodist chapel in nearby Seneca Falls, New York. They didn't have much time to get the word out. And yet, somehow three hundred women and men from across the Northeast, including Garrison and the rising star of the abolition movement — a self-liberated former slave named Frederick Douglass — found their way to Seneca Falls.

Stanton welcomed the guests, then introduced Mott, who gave a stirring address. One attendee remembered Mott as "the moving spirit of the occasion."

After she spoke, Stanton returned to the podium to read a statement she had written called the Declaration of Sentiments.

Its words were familiar to everyone in attendance.

"We hold these truths to be self-evident," she read, "that all men and women are created equal." *And women.*

The document continued in this way, using the language of the Declaration of Independence to express the many grievances that women had against male authority:

"He has never permitted her to exercise her inalienable right to the elective franchise.

"He has compelled her to submit to laws, in the formation of which she had no voice.

"He has denied her the facilities for obtaining a thorough education — all colleges being closed against her."

And so on.

The Declaration of Sentiments made but one demand. It was simple yet astounding: Women were to be given "immediate admission to all the rights and privileges which belong to them as citizens of these United States."

For the next two days the attendees sweltered in the stuffy chapel. Yet as word of the convention spread, people kept coming. At last the balcony was overflowing. The Declaration of Sentiments would be re-read, discussed, and amended. At the convention's end, it would be signed by one hundred of the three hundred persons present — 68 women and 32 men.

What would happen next? No one was sure, but the Declaration's last line provided a clue about the women's strategy:

"We hope this Convention will be followed by a series of Conventions, embracing every part of the country."

Seneca Falls was held partly in reaction to the 1840 anti-slavery convention attended by (clockwise from top left) Elizabeth Cady Stanton, William Lloyd Garrison, and Lucretia Mott, whose sister Martha Wright (bottom left) also planned the convention.

Coming Out

Meanwhile in Vermont, Clarina Nichols seemed to be growing bolder by the day. "I know some folks argue that because women's physical power ain't so strong and won't hold out so long as men's at any bodily labor, her mind can't be that strong," Deborah Van Winkle wrote one day in the *Windham County Democrat*.

"But God and the angels and glorified spirits ain't got no bodies nor physical powers at all! And I reckon that's proof enough that women may have as much intellect as good men."

Mrs. Van Winkle was a feminist! And through her voice, Clarina began speaking up for women's rights in the mid-1840s, even before the historic meeting at Seneca Falls.

Mass movements often explode onto the scene, seemingly out

of nowhere. In reality they are the result of years of quiet ferment, often bubbling just below the surface. That was the case with the world's first women's rights movement.

First the women had to get their feet wet, organizing for a moral cause. For Clarina and thousands of other women, the cause was temperance. For others it was anti-slavery. Next, they had to get comfortable expressing their thoughts in words. Then they had to learn how to organize like-minded women to lead petition drives and lobby their husbands and friends for change.

Finally, they had to be bold enough to step out on stage and make their case before gatherings of men and women. There was a strong social custom against women speaking in mixed-sex meetings. Men were known to stand up and leave the room whenever this happened. Others would stay in their seats and heckle any woman brave enough to speak up.

Clarina heard about a minister who was conducting a ladies' Bible study. Because he was a man and they were women, the minister declared that this was a "promiscuous" meeting, one that involved both men and women. In such settings it would be improper for any of the women to speak her own thoughts. He did allow one exception, however: A woman could respond if she spoke entirely in Bible verses. What a strange "discussion" this would be to anyone passing by, Clarina thought.

But the time was coming for Nichols herself to speak up and stop hiding behind Deborah Van Winkle. Whether it was the Van Winkle columns, or just women talking amongst themselves, Clarina became a magnet for women in distress. Women stopped her on the street to tell her their woes. Others wrote her

WINDHAM COUNTY DEMOCRAT.

EDITED BY MRS C. I. H. NICHOLS.

Brattleboro, Vt., March 2, 1853.

The Paupers' Removal.

"It isn't a *woman's* vocation to write politics; her sphere is at home," says one and another, and we always say *amen*. 'Astonished' are you, gentle reader? And did you think that Mrs Nichols "meddles with politics" because she finds their details congenial with her tastes, or for any reason but that politics *meddle* with the happiness of home and its most sacred relations, with *woman* and all that is dearest to the affections and hopes of a true woman? If you dreamed that politics have any hold upon our sympathies not strictly belonging to their power over the *homes* of the land for weal or woe—any claim upon our time and efforts not identified with our own home interests, you have done us grievous wrong, dear reader, and we pray you just listen to a brief chapter of state policy which was forced upon our notice, a few days since, and say if women, as the "guardian angels" of the "*sanctity* of home" and the "inviolableness of the home relations," have not a call to *write* politics, to *talk* politics?

Only after she had been running the *Windham County Democrat* for several years did Clarina decide to publish her name in its pages. She feared ridicule from the men in town — and rightly so.

long letters pouring out the details of their difficult lives. "I am a walking storehouse of facts on the subject of woman's wrongs," she confided to a friend.

For her, it always came back to property. Once a woman said "I do," she may as well have added, "I do hand over to my husband my property, my money, and all my earthly possessions. He may do with them as he wishes." The quilt her mother made for her, the horse her father gave her, the wedding dress she bought with her own earnings — all of these now belonged, legally, to her husband. He could sell, gamble, or give them away. His wife could object, but she had no legal standing. In the eyes of the law she did not exist. She was under her husband's protection, and her husband spoke and decided for both of them.

Nothing showed that more clearly than the legal status of her name. A woman might be known as Mary White all her life, but when she married that name disappeared. Now she was Mrs. Henry Jones. If a wife was fortunate, her husband was kind, wise, and loving. Wives who had chosen poorly or hastily, those whose husbands changed for the worse after marriage — these women had few options.

If a wife could not convince her husband with reason, tears, anger, affection, deceit, flattery, or coaxing, she was out of luck. A husband had the legal right to have his way, to demand sex, and to discipline his wife if she didn't carry out his wishes or please him in some way he deemed vital. For most men, male authority was a source of pride, for even the poorest man could claim to be lord of his castle.

Clarina Nichols came to believe that married women could never achieve security for themselves and their children unless they had the legal right to own and control their own property and wages.

She would ponder these things at night while reading her stack of exchange papers. Lately, a number of these newspapers arriving at the *Democrat's* office were edited by women like her. And these editors were putting their names on the masthead: Amelia Bloomer, Jane Swisshelm, Lydia Jane Pierson. It gave her courage to know that other women were starting to "do and dare for the cause of humanity," Nichols recalled later.

In early 1847, she began to write about women and property.

New York State had tried to pass a bill through its legislature in 1846 granting married women control over their own property. Vermont needed to take up the cause as well. Clarina argued in the *Democrat* that a married woman needed legal protection "to fill 'woman's sphere' [her role] as wife and mother."

Nichols' whole life had been leading up to this moment. From the stories of the broken women who had shown up at her house when she was a girl, to her own terror after learning that Justin had made off with their children, to the sad stories of women she carried in her heart, she felt deeply the injustice of a world in which men controlled women — right down to the last stitch of their clothing.

And at least one reader of the *Windham County Democrat* felt the injustice as well. This reader happened to sit in the Vermont state legislature. Inspired by Nichols' articles, he introduced Vermont's first married women's property rights bill in 1847. This bill did not go as far as Nichols would have liked it to go, but it was a start. And more importantly, it passed and became law. It was a small victory in what would be a long war. Nichols called the bill "the first breath" of life for married women in Vermont.

By 1850 the *Windham County Democrat* was selling 1,000 copies a week throughout the Northeast. Clarina and George no longer had to rely on their political base for support. Ever since Deborah Van Winkle had appeared in its pages, however, the *Democrat's* opponents had started to wonder if George Nichols was making all the decisions at his newspaper. Why would he write a column in a woman's voice? Around town, people began to whisper that Mr. Nichols was letting Mrs. Nichols run the newspaper.

Although Clarina enjoyed sparring with her critics in print, she was still reluctant about the idea of debating them on the streets of Brattleboro. She had yet to announce her role at the paper, and the masthead of the *Democrat* continued to credit her husband as both editor and publisher.

Finally, an editor at a rival newspaper published an editorial that challenged her to step out of the shadows. He reported hearing a funny rumor that a woman was running the *Democrat*. Such a thing was impossible, he declared, for a woman was completely incapable of managing a political newspaper for herself. Mrs. Nichols, he insisted, was merely carrying out the orders of her sick husband.

That did it. The following week Clarina published an article in the *Democrat* revealing that she was its editor, that she had been carrying on its editorial and publishing duties for several years, and that her husband trusted her fully to make important decisions about the newspaper by herself. From that time on, the masthead of the *Democrat* read: EDITED BY MRS. C. I. H. NICHOLS.

"My husband wanted me to come forward before," she told a friend later on, "but I wanted to make sure that I had gained men's confidence in my abilities to run a political newspaper." Truth be told, she needed confidence in her own abilities as well. Fortunately, other women just like herself were starting to speak up all across the North.

Worcester

I n the summer of 1850, a call was issued for the First National Woman's Rights Convention. It was to be held that October in Worcester, Massachusetts. A printed copy of the notice arrived in Brattleboro. Clarina read it hungrily.

"The signs are encouraging; the time is opportune," it read. "Come, then, to this Convention. It is your duty, if you are worthy of your age and country. Give the help of your best thought to separate the light from the darkness."

How could she not go?

Worcester was chosen because it was the railroad hub of New England. Twenty-four trains passed through there each day. All through Tuesday, October 22, hundreds of excited reformers, curiosity-seekers, and reporters poured into the city.

Abby Price, who spoke at the 1850 convention, lived in the Hopedale community. Its members tried to model a "practical Christianity" that opposed war, private property, and separate "spheres" for men and women.

The next morning, 1,000 attendees filled Brinley Hall. "The room was crowded to excess, every seat and aisle and the space around the platform being filled, men and women standing on their feet," reported the *New-York Tribune*. One reformer had come all the way from California for the big meeting.

The chief organizer of the First National Woman's Rights Convention was a wealthy New Englander named Paulina Wright Davis. She had created a sensation with her lectures on female anatomy. This was a taboo subject for proper ladies. Women did not undress even for their doctors. Davis, however, toured the Northeast with her companion, a mannequin on which she pointed out women's reproductive organs.

Other women at the convention were also comfortable speaking in front of a crowd. Some, like Lucretia Mott, had faced down angry pro-slavery mobs. But most of the women who gathered that day had no speaking experience. Certainly not in a room that big. Many were timid and soft-spoken. Time and again, audience members would have to tell the woman up at the podium:

Speak up!

Several ladies were so nervous, they trembled as they spoke. Others looked like they were going to faint. But they too found courage as a still small voice inside urged them onward:

Speak up!

Of course they were inexperienced at speaking before crowds. That was why they were meeting, so that they would all learn, together, to *speak up.*

At the end, everyone agreed that all of the speakers, even the ones who had been hard to hear, were quite eloquent.

Among the speakers at the 1850 convention was Abby Price, who lived in nearby Hopedale with a utopian community that was committed to gender equality. "In many countries we see women reduced to the condition of a slave," Price said. "In others she is dressed up as a mere plaything for [men's] amusement."

She said most young women could look forward to nothing better than "mindless factory work or half-paid work as seam-stresses, hat-makers, or typesetters." What Price believed in was equality between the sexes. She called it "co-sovereignty."

Over the course of two days the members of the First National Woman's Rights Convention passed several resolutions:

Women should have equal access to education and jobs.

Women should receive equal pay for equal work.

Married women should be able to hold and control property in their own names.

Mothers should have equal custody rights in cases of divorce.

Women should be allowed to vote.

The delegates claimed these rights not only for themselves but for "the million and a half of slave women at the South." In this way they tied the new women's movement to the anti-slavery movement where so many of them had gotten their start.

Clarina Nichols signed the resolutions along with 260 other women and men.

As editor of a newspaper, Nichols was one of the most accomplished women there. Very quickly she began making friends with the delegates and organizers of the convention. They asked her to sit on committees. And then they elected her one of five vice-presidents who would serve the following year, when the Second National Woman's Rights Convention would be again held in Worcester.

Her days as a behind-the-scenes, anonymous editor were over. In no time at all, Clarina Nichols had become a leader in the world's first women's rights movement. And in another year she too would be stepping onto the stage of Brinley Hall and speaking up for women's rights.

She was completely taken by everything that was going on around her. In later years she would recall a moment during the convention when she had to return to her room and lie down, just to calm her racing heart. Clarina was excited — and for very good reason. This was a large sisterhood. And there was a place for her in it.

Clarina Speaks Up

On October 15, 1851, the noted abolitionist Wendell Phillips took the hand of Clarina Nichols and led her to the podium. A thousand delegates and a gaggle of newspaper reporters awaited her words. It was the first time she had given a public address since graduating from Timothy Cressy's private school in Vermont.

She must have hesitated, for her escort leaned over and whispered in her ear, "You must speak now, Mrs. Nichols."

She had no law degree, but Nichols had studied law intently on her own. From an early age she realized that the law discriminated against women, and she had a good idea of how it should be changed. She also knew that most people had little idea what the law said, or why it was so important for women in the movement to understand abstract legal concepts.

As Nichols prepared her speech, she thought of people she had known over the years who had suffered great injustices because of their sex. Her audience might forget the words, but she made sure they would not forget her stories.

She spoke for one hour. Later, she would claim that she had not prepared much ahead of time. To her listeners, however, it was clear that she had indeed prepared very carefully.

She began by telling her audience about a woman she had known who was married to a humble farmer. One day the farmer became seriously ill. He was too weak to do all the chores himself and too poor to pay a laborer to help him out. So the farmer's wife went out into the field. She helped her husband move a pile of heavy logs so that he could plant his crops.

Would anyone criticize this woman for going out of her womanly sphere? It was easy to talk about "man's sphere" and "woman's sphere" when times were good.

"If I were a wife and loved my husband, I, too, would help him when he needed help," Nichols declared. "What true-hearted woman would not do the same?"

This, she told her audience, would be the major theme of her talk. "I shall say very little of woman's rights," she assured them. "Instead I would impress upon you woman's responsibilities."

In fact, the whole talk would be about woman's rights. But it was a shrewd choice of words. Most people in 1851 weren't sure that women needed more rights. If they saw, however, that they needed rights to carry out their womanly duties, they might change their minds.

Clarina believed that Americans valued fairness. So she filled her speech with stories of women who were treated unfairly under the law. No story was more heartbreaking than the one she told about a self-made woman she knew in West Townshend.

This woman, who was unmarried much of her life, worked hard and saved her money. By middle age she had accumulated a nice nest egg for herself. Then she married. Her new husband had a good reputation, but no money of his own. He was a widower with children who were grown and living elsewhere. The woman used her savings to buy herself and her new husband a cozy cottage, where she hoped to spend many pleasant years together.

But then her husband died — and by the property laws of that era, his grown children were awarded *two-thirds of the woman's estate*. The widow was entitled to only one-third of the cottage ... that she had bought with her own money! Furthermore, she could not sell the cottage, even if she desperately needed the money. And she did need the money, because most of her estate had been given away to her husband's children.

As Nichols told this sad tale, she could hear a murmur rippling through the audience. It seemed everyone in Brinley Hall had known a neighbor or loved one whose story reminded them of this widow's plight.

But there was more to tell. One day, when she was quite old, the widow was found in her bed, unable to move — paralyzed. She would remain paralyzed until the end of her life, three years later.

"And now, friends, how did the laws support and protect this poor widow?" Nichols asked her hearers. Even with a capacity

This magazine cartoon, sketched at a May 1859 women's rights convention, pokes fun at the idea of a woman speaking in public — but also shows that such talks were very popular with both women and men.

audience of 1,000 people, she probably could have spoken in a normal voice. Everyone was on the edge of their seats, waiting for her next words.

"I will tell you," she declared. "They set her up at auction, and struck her off [sold her] to the man who had a heart to keep her at the cheapest rate! Three years!" That was how the government dealt with poor widows in Clarina's day. It held an auction, and the man who offered the lowest price won. The town would then pay this man to provide minimum care to the needy person. There was no incentive to provide good care. The less he spent on the widow the more he had for himself.

When the widow died, she received the cheapest ceremony as well, a pauper's burial. What was left of her estate "was divided, as had been the other two-thirds, among her husband's well-to-do children."

A reporter on the scene wrote down what happened next: *"Great sensation."*

After the room had calmed down, Nichols shifted her talk to address the men in the audience. She was going to tell them a few things they needed to hear — things that women had rarely, if ever, been given the chance to tell them in public.

"Oh, men! In the enjoyment of well-secured property rights, you beautify your snug homesteads," she said, "and it never occurs to you that no such blissful feeling of security finds rest in the bosom of your wives."

To illustrate how clueless men could be, Clarina told a story about a husband who was filling out his will one night. He called his wife into the room.

"My dear, I have been thinking that the care of a third of my estate will be a burden to you," he told her. The husband proposed, instead, leaving all the money with their grown male children.

"The boys will supply you," he assured her. "You can trust our boys to do right."

"Oh yes, my dear," his wife replied, "we have excellent boys." But, she added, "we have other children, and differences obtain in their circumstances." This was the wife's way of reminding her husband that they had raised "excellent" girls as well. The mother did not want to see them cheated out of their inheritance. She wanted to control her husband's estate after he was gone so she

68

could help any of their children, male or female.

"When one and another have needed, you have opened your purse and given them help," she reminded her husband. "When you are gone there may still occur these opportunities for aiding them, and I should be glad to have it in my power to do as you have done."

Give me power to do what you have done.

It was such a simple argument. Through storytelling, Nichols put skin on her arguments. In a dozen ways she told the men in the audience that what women wanted was exactly the same thing men wanted — the power to control their lives, their money, and their property.

She even shared her own story of being left "the sole parent of sons by a first marriage." Once she married George, "the law says that, having married again, I am a legal nonentity [non-person] ... therefore I shall not be their guardian." Even if a mother had been her children's legal guardian for years, she lost that status the moment she remarried. The new husband may not even have known his new wife's children. Why should he suddenly become their legal guardian? Were not such laws totally absurd? Nichols raised her voice: "I appeal to every man who has lived a half century, [is] the mother not the most faithful guardian of her children's interests?"

Give me power so that I may protect my children.

She piled on the examples, unloading them as though she had waited a lifetime to unburden herself.

She told about the time she was traveling from New York home to Vermont in 1833. A gentleman came over and introduced her to a weary-looking woman who was traveling with him.

"She was born here," the gentleman said, "the mother of two young children, with no means of support but her earnings. She was a capable girl." Unfortunately, the woman had married badly. "Her husband in a few years became a drunkard and a brute, neglected his business, and expended their entire living," the gentleman explained.

The wife took the children and moved around New York, looking for work. "But he pursued her from place to place," Nichols said, "collecting her wages by process of law, and taking possession of every garment not on her own or children's persons."

Finally, some friends took pity on the woman, "with her hatless and shoeless children," and bought them all tickets to New Hampshire. The gentleman wanted Clarina to make sure the family made it safely there. Why New Hampshire? Because "a year's residence should enable her to procure a divorce." In her situation, that was the best possible outcome she could hope for.

"Now, friends," Nichols told her audience, "if under New York laws this poor woman had enjoyed legal control of her own earnings, she might have retained her first home, supported her children, and — happy as a mother — endured hopefully."

Give me power so that I may raise my children.

Paulina Wright Davis later recalled that people in the audience were weeping during the speech, including "many eyes all unused to tears." Clarina Nichols had wanted to make dull and dry legal problems come alive, and she had succeeded.

Nichols ended her talk with a challenge to the young women in the room. It was time to stop spending hours every day obsess-

> # WOMAN'S RIGHTS TRACTS,..No. 6.
>
> ## ON THE
>
> # RESPONSIBILITIES OF WOMAN.
>
> ## A SPEECH BY MRS. C. I. H. NICHOLS,
>
> ### WORCESTER, OCT. 15, 1851.
>
> Mrs. C. I. H. Nichols, of Brattleboro', Vt., then came forward and spoke as follows :—
>
> My friends, I have made no preparation to address you. I left home feeling that if I had anything to do here, I should have the grace given me to do it; or if there should be any branch of the subject not sufficiently presented, I would present it. And now, friends, in following so many speakers, who have so well occupied the ground, I will come as a gleaner, and be as a Ruth among my fellow-laborers.
>
> I commenced life with the most refined notions of woman's sphere. My pride of womanhood lay within this ...

Nichols' first speech was immediately rushed into print, which is fortunate for us — it is the only surviving speech of hers that we have.

ing over beauty and looks. "These address themselves to man's lower nature — his passions," she told them. "And when age has robbed you of the one, and him of the other, you are left unloved and unlovely! Cultivate, then, your powers of mind and heart."

And then she told one last very personal story.

"When a young girl of 14, I said to my father, 'Give me education' ... [for] if I marry, and am poor in this world's goods, I can educate my children myself. If my husband should be unfortunate, the sheriff can take his goods. But *no creditor* can attach the capital invested *here!*"

Clarina tapped her forehead.

And the crowd went wild.

Of the hundreds of speeches Nichols would deliver over the next two decades, this one — titled "On the Responsibilities of Woman" — would be her most famous. The women's rights movement quickly turned this speech into a pamphlet that was widely distributed.

Nichols would change her approach in the coming years. She began to argue for women's rights, not because mothers needed equal rights in order to raise their children, but because all women, married or not, deserved the full rights of citizenship.

And yet, "The Responsibilities of Woman" lays out the agenda that would occupy Clarina Nichols for the rest of her life: property rights for married women, control of wages, custody rights, reform of inheritance laws, equal educational and vocational opportunities for females — and in one brief passage, the right of women to vote. More importantly, it established a method of arguing for women's rights that would be identified with her for the rest of her life. It was never a harsh or heavy-handed approach, but used humor and reason to persuade men that granting women equality was a win for both sexes.

"Only those who have suffered as I have can have the courage and determination to move steadily forward against [the] opposition," she said in later years. "And if people like this give up, the work of reform is hopeless."

Gaining Courage

The women's rights movement would soon become identified with just one cause: suffrage. In the beginning, though, there were many ideas about where the movement should be directing its energies. At Seneca Falls and Worcester, women were speaking up for the very first time. And they had a lot on their minds! It took a few years for the women's movement to sort out the various issues and decide that suffrage — the right to vote — was the most important right that could be won. With suffrage, women could elect the legislators who could change the laws under which women suffered.

In 1852, a new face emerged who would become the leading advocate for suffrage. Susan B. Anthony was an expert anti-slav-

Susan B. Anthony in 1852, the year she joined the women's rights movement.

ery organizer who had decided to devote herself to the women's movement after reading some of the speeches given at the 1850 Worcester convention.

After the pamphlet on "The Responsibilities of Woman" had been published, Anthony wrote Nichols and asked her to speak at a meeting in New York. Clarina had to decline — in addition to her newspaper duties, she was already in great demand due to her speech at the convention — but she sent Anthony issues of the *Democrat*. That was the beginning of a friendship that would last more than 30 years.

These two women had much in common. Both had gotten their start in the temperance movement. Each had felt the sting of earning only half of what men earned as schoolteachers. Nichols was brimming with stories of women who had been mistreated by the law. Anthony knew all too well the shoddy treatment of female teachers. And now, within 18 months of each other, they were committing to the women's rights movement with every fiber in their bodies.

"It is most invigorating to watch the development of a woman in the work for humanity," Nichols wrote Anthony in April 1852. But, she added, her friend should be aware of the stages that every woman goes through as she learns how to speak up for her rights.

"First," Clarina said, the new activist is "anxious for the cause and depressed with a sense of her own inability; next, partial success of timid efforts creating a hope; next, a faith; and then the fruition of complete self-devotion.

"Such will be your history," Nichols predicted.

By 1852 newspapers were beginning to pay attention to the new women's rights movement. Some were fair. But many newspapers treated the movement as a joke. Instead of focusing on the message, reporters would focus on the women's looks. They called the women "unsexed" and "freaks of nature." They suggested these were not ladies but "she-men," anything but true women. They printed cartoons that showed women with bulging muscles and masculine features — square jaws, receding hairlines, beards, and moustaches.

Big-city newspapers practiced this kind of rough, take-no-prisoners brand of journalism all the time. But the men who wrote the stories and published the cartoons were used to it. This was their arena. They had written the rules. And if the women were expecting to be treated more courteously because of their sex, they were greatly mistaken.

Still, there was an especially cruel edge to the sexist coverage of the women's rights movement. And there was no better sign of this than in the huge ruckus that was raised over a new piece of ladies' clothing that had arrived on the scene.

They were called bloomers.

Named for Amelia Bloomer, who promoted the fashion heavily in her newspaper *The Lily*, bloomers were knee-length skirts or dresses worn over a pair of trousers cuffed at the ankle. Bloomers gave women freedom of movement while still wearing skirts. They were amazed at how comfortable the new fashion was and what a difference it made in how they could move. Bloomers made women feel as free as young boys.

At first, male opinion about bloomers was divided. A factory owner in Massachusetts who employed mostly young women urged them to switch to bloomers, which were less likely to become caught in the machinery. Amelia Bloomer relentlessly promoted the fashion throughout 1851 as a healthy alternative to longer dresses.

But then, opinion quickly turned. The press began to rain insult and ridicule down on "Bloomerism." Nichols began to hear reports of young men who would circle any bloomer-wearing woman they saw walking down the street and verbally abuse her.

In the *Democrat,* she carried on a debate for weeks with a rival newspaper editor about bloomers. "We can't understand how shortening women's skirts will cause such dreadful mischief," she

Newspaper editor Amelia Bloomer did not invent them, but her promotion of a dress-over-pantaloons style inspired the "Bloomer craze." She modeled them in this illustration from *The Lily* in 1851.

wrote. She pointed out that the style had been worn in various places for centuries and until its recent association with Bloomer had been known as "the Turkish dress."

If men were truly interested in female modesty, Nichols tartly added, maybe the critics should worry as much about inches taken from the *top* of an outfit as much as from the bottom. She was referring to the plunging necklines that revealed a much more delicate part of a female's anatomy than bloomers did.

Her opponent argued that the Bible was against women wearing trousers and predicted great evil would come from the new fashion. Long skirts, he wrote, made women act like women were supposed to act — modest and refined.

Nichols fired back that if that was the case, perhaps men should be forced to wear long skirts for a while. Maybe men would be better behaved, and women who chose to wear bloomers would no longer have to fear "being molested by rowdy and obscene jeers."

But it was a lost cause. Bloomers took center stage in the discussion of women's rights. They were a political statement in their own way, but there were much more important things the women wanted to talk about. And so, by late 1852 most women in the movement went back to wearing long skirts, at least in public.

Nichols could only shake her head in wonder. If men were so concerned about wearing pants, she once said, maybe instead of the bald eagle the national symbol should be a pair of trousers.

Vermont men may not have been ready to see their women in bloomers. But Nichols hoped they might be ready to allow women to vote in school elections. After all, what could be more womanly than an interest in schools and children?

Like the others in the movement, she had started to see how suffrage was central to the women's rights cause. Women, she realized, would never be taken seriously until they could vote.

And she saw school suffrage as a good starting point. It would get men used to the idea of women voting. They would see that the Earth did not spin off its axis if democracy included the fairer sex.

In 1852 Nichols collected 200 signatures on a petition that she circulated around Brattleboro. The petition asked that women be granted school voting rights. Opponents fired back, saying the *Democrat* should be shut down or sold.

She did not take the threat lightly. Neither did her friends. On October 27, 1852, she printed a letter of support from "Many Citizens." The letter said that, while the *Democrat* might be a little heavy on the women's rights issue, it was under Mrs. Nichols' guidance a "good family paper" that "speaks out fearlessly for good morals and the highest interest of humanity."

The newspaper spoke out fearlessly. But would the editor?

She would soon have her chance. A friend managed to get her an appointment to speak to the state legislature. This was her chance to present her petition to the ruling body of Vermont.

She asked George if she should do it.

"Have you the nerve?" he asked.

It was the right question to ask. Up until then she had only spoken before friendly crowds. These legislators might be polite, or they might be skeptical — maybe even rowdy. In fact, one of them had already declared, "If the lady wants to make herself ridiculous, let her come and make herself as ridiculous as possible and as soon as possible."

In the end, though, she could not pass up the opportunity to be the first woman to address the Vermont legislature.

She stepped to the podium and began. Then she stopped suddenly and rested her head in her hand. One observer thought she was about to faint. But Nichols quickly pulled herself together and went on to deliver her speech.

Her fiercest opponent had planned to present her with a pair of men's trousers. Men often said that women's rights leaders wanted to "wear the pants in the family." The legislator wanted to embarrass Nichols and get everyone laughing, instead of thinking about what she had just said. Clarina must have known he was up to something because she turned and addressed him directly after her speech. She said she had bought the dress she was wearing that day using her own money. And yet, legally it belonged to her husband. This was not because he wanted to own it, but because of "a law adopted by bachelors and other women's husbands." Perhaps, she told him, men shouldn't tease women about wanting to wear men's pants until they had given up the right to own women's skirts!

For a moment there was silence. Then came the "muffled thunder of stamping feet," as the legislators showed their appreciation for their quick-witted guest. The trousers were never presented.

A crowd of excited women waited for her afterwards. They had listened in the galleries to the first speech on women's rights that many of them had ever heard. One of them gave Clarina a friendly handshake.

"We did not know before what woman's rights were, Mrs. Nichols," she said, smiling broadly, "but we are for woman's rights!"

The legislature did not act on her petition, but she had won in the court of public opinion. One newspaper that was hostile to her cause remarked that Mrs. Nichols had been unable to "unsex" herself while making her case to the legislature. Clarina took this as a compliment.

The World Is on the Move

I n the fall of 1853 thousands of visitors from home and abroad descended on New York City. They were there to see the first World's Fair ever held on American soil. The city's 92 hotels were booked and its streets jammed with coaches, omnibuses, and hacks. The sidewalks were crowded with fairgoers in a festive mood and vendors selling everything from sausages to pickled eggs.

The main attraction was the Crystal Palace, built especially for the fair to house thousands of industrial exhibits and inventions. An enormous structure of iron and glass designed in the shape of a Greek cross, the Crystal Palace shimmered at night, lit from the inside by hundreds of gas lanterns.

The organizers of the World's Fair had no less a purpose than

New York's Crystal Palace, site of the 1853 World's Fair, was inspired by the Crystal Palace in London, where the first global exhibition was held in 1851.

bringing about world peace. They were not alone. The editors of the city's newest paper, the *New York Times*, said that the technologies showcased at the fair, like the telegraph and the safety elevator, would unite the world.

"The Crystal Palace is a symbol of the might of Man," the *Times* editorialized. "Look on, ye Nations, and vow eternal peace and justice."

Clarina Nichols may well have visited the Crystal Palace — it was, after all, the talk of the town — but she and thousands of fellow reformers had come to New York for other reasons. Two temperance conventions, an anti-slavery meeting, and a women's rights convention were being held back-to-back-to-back that September. It was a huge moment for American reformers. They were feeling more optimistic than ever.

There was a popular song at that time which expressed the mood perfectly:

The world is on the move —
look about, look about!
There is much we may improve —
do not doubt, do not doubt!
Let us onward, then, for right
(nothing more, nothing more)
And let justice be the might
we adore, we adore.
Build no hopes upon the sand!
For a people hand-in-hand
can make this a better land
than before, than before!

Not everyone shared the good feelings. An unruly mob nearly took over the women's rights convention. Newspaper reporters filled pages with unflattering portraits of the reformers. Perhaps most surprising was the reaction of people inside the temperance movement. This was where many of the women had gotten their start in political organizing. But a large faction of the temperance movement was openly hostile to the new women's cause.

The trouble had started in an organizing meeting the previous spring. The World's Temperance Convention had denied Susan B. Anthony a seat on their business committee. If there was one woman qualified to serve on a business committee, it was she. Anthony had a reputation throughout the reform community as a superb organizer. She was also a precise bookkeeper. And yet, a majority of men voted not only to keep Anthony off the committee. They voted to bar all women from participating.

Elizabeth Cady Stanton, Lucretia Mott, and William Lloyd Garrison couldn't believe it. This was exactly what had happened to them in 1840 at the World Anti-Slavery Convention in London. For good measure, the temperance delegates also refused to admit Dr. James McCune Smith because he was black.

Outraged, the women and their male allies marched out. They organized their own gathering — the *Whole* World's Temperance Convention. At this meeting no one was excluded on the basis of sex or race. Quickly the public turned its attention away from the "Half-World" temperance meeting to this one.

America's most progressive men and women turned out in force at the Whole World's Temperance Convention. Anthony was appointed secretary. From her seat on the podium, Clarina Nichols looked over the proceedings with a roster of all-star vice presidents. They included Lucretia Mott, the Reverend Antoinette Brown, firebrand Lucy Stone, showman P.T. Barnum, Horace Greeley of the *New-York Tribune*, and Sherman Booth, the Milwaukee newspaper editor who had earned fame for violating the 1850 Fugitive Slave Law. (He had aided an escaping slave and served jail time.) The reporter for Greeley's *Tribune* pointed out that there were fewer men on stage than women. The reporter approved of the new ratio.

Two thousand reformers cheered one speaker after the next. A popular musical group, the Amphions, entertained with such crowd-pleasers as "The World Is on the Move," "Dawn of the

Good Time Coming," and "The Temperance War Song." The delegates were told that the wind was shifting and that victory was in sight. The world would soon be free of the effects of alcohol. Sober citizens would end slavery. Domestic abuse and poverty would be a thing of the past. And women would take their rightful place in society. It was a glorious vision.

Many speakers declared that all three causes were intertwined. Temperance could not be separated from women's rights and the abolition of slavery. Freedom for the enslaved, rights for women, and a drug-free world — these were three strands of one strong cord.

The original goal of the temperance movement had been to convince people to swear off alcohol. Thousands of Americans had already signed temperance pledges. But now the sons and daughters of temperance wanted to do more than save individuals. They believed they could save society as a whole. Cut off the sources of alcohol, they said. Get to the root of the problem and there will be no alcoholism. Inns and "grog shops" where alcohol was served were threatened or closed down. Barrels of whisky were dumped in the streets. Some temperance supporters had even gone so far as to chop down apple orchards when they thought the apples would be made into hard cider.

Nichols was introduced at the convention to loud applause.

"I say that woman is the greatest sufferer," she declared as she listed all the ways in which the law gave husbands — even the drunkards who caused nothing but trouble — complete control over their wives and children.

The *Tribune* reporter described the gathering as "the most spirited and able Convention on temperance that was ever held. It has already done good, and cannot fail to do more."

On the Sunday before the opening of the women's convention, the Anti-Slavery Society held its meeting. Later in the day Antoinette Brown, the first woman ordained by a mainline Protestant church in the United States, preached a public sermon. Five thousand people were reported in attendance.

"We saw, in broad daylight, in a public hall in the city of New York, a gathering of unsexed women," wrote the correspondent for the New York *Herald*, a newspaper that never met a reform movement it liked. The *Herald* spent more time reporting on what the attendees wore than on what Reverend Brown said.

Next came the women's convention — and this one was the wildest of them all.

The days were already warm, but the sight of so many "strong-minded" women around New York City raised the temperature several more degrees. Some were wearing bloomers and suffering for their choice of clothing. As so often happened, packs of young men would surround bloomer-wearing females on the street, taunting and teasing, even shoving them.

Anyone with 25 cents could attend the women's rights convention. Between 2,000 and 3,000 people crowded into the Broadway Tabernacle, whose galleries looked down unto a large stage. Every seat on the floor was taken, and the galleries were packed.

Scores of young men fanned out across the audience for the purpose of raising a ruckus. They hung over the balconies, called

The Broadway Tabernacle held three thousand people "in the round." Everyone could hear the speaker if the crowd kept quiet.

out to one another across the hall, swigged alcohol from flasks concealed in their jackets, and began to boo and heckle every speaker who came to the podium. The women suspected that the young men had been recruited by older "establishment" men to do their dirty work, but this was never proven.

Antoinette Brown was drowned out with cries of "Shut up!" "Time's up!" and "We don't want to hear you!"

Ernestine Rose, an organizer of the event, called in the police and demanded they cart off the rowdies. "The mayor promised to see that our meeting should not be disturbed, and I call upon him to keep order," she said. "As citizens of New York we have a right to this protection, for we pay our money for it!"

When that did little good, Rose called on the members themselves to help restore order. Greeley and other male delegates tussled with the troublemakers and dragged a few of them out.

Nichols, feeling no fear at this point, launched into one of her favorite topics: the wronged widow and the woman whose husband had left her and taken their children.

"In the Green Mountain State a great many sermons have lately been preached on the text, 'Wives, submit yourselves to your husbands,' " she told the noisy room. But what if the husband was a "woman's rights man"? What if he wanted her to enjoy the same rights as he enjoyed? "My husband wishes me to vote," she declared. If this was her husband's wish, who could say she was opposing the will of God?

One of the speakers that stood up to the rowdies was Sojourner Truth, an ex-slave who had already shown that she would not be intimidated by anyone. At an earlier convention Truth had responded powerfully to a minister when he argued that the Bible commanded men to rule over women. "Where did your Christ come from?" Truth shot back. "From God and a woman! Man had *nothing* to do with Him."

Now, Sojourner Truth pulled herself to her full six-foot height and crossed to the podium. At the sight of this tall, confident black woman, the rowdies increased the volume of their whoops, hollers, and jeers.

"You may hiss as much as you like, but it's coming," she declared. "We'll have our rights. See if we don't! And you can't stop us from them — see if you can!"

Both days of the convention ended in total uproar. The "mob

convention," as it came to be called, won sympathy for women and new interest in the women's rights cause. The bad behavior of the young rowdies, combined with the snub from the Half-World Convention, made some men reconsider. Perhaps these women had a point. Perhaps they should listen a little more carefully.

Writing in Garrison's newspaper *The Liberator*, Nichols reported that "several gentlemen" had publicly apologized at the women's convention. One of these was Isaac C. Pray, a poet and contributor to a leading New York journal. He told the women he was sorry for his attempts to make the women's rights cause look ridiculous. He now believed their cause "was from God and bound to succeed." The women gave him heartfelt applause and invited him into their fold. Nichols wrote that Pray's "whole appearance and language proved him a man, both good and courageous."

The women had shown some courage themselves, managing to conduct a convention over the continuous yelling and interruptions of the rowdies. What had been in doubt just three years earlier was now a widely accepted fact: Women's rights could take its place alongside abolition and temperance as one of the great reforms of the age.

During her time in New York, Clarina was approached by Horace Greeley with an offer. Would she go to Wisconsin on behalf of the New York State Temperance Society? There was a need for a strong speaker to tour the new state in favor of a total temperance law that was on the ballot that November. She had promoted a similar law in Vermont.

Most people outside the big Eastern cities had never heard a woman speak. That in itself would draw crowds. Would she go?

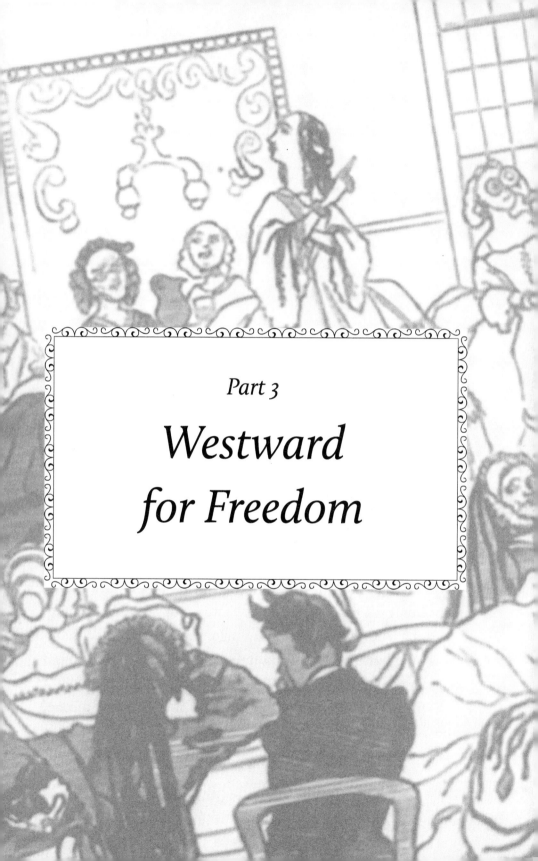

Part 3

Westward for Freedom

Winning Wisconsin

Though George Nichols was in poor health, he urged his wife to make the long trip to Wisconsin. "You will be doing just the work you love and enjoying a journey which you otherwise could not afford," he said. His daughters promised to look after him in Clarina's absence.

Nichols' partner in Wisconsin was Lydia Fowler, one of the first female doctors in the United States and the first woman to teach at a medical college. Their assignment was to tour Wisconsin, giving lectures that supported a temperance bill that would go before the voters in November.

Each night Fowler would lecture on the dangers of alcohol from a medical point of view. Then Nichols would take the stage and talk about how alcoholism affected the family, a subject she

Nichols and Lydia Fowler traveled west using two forms of transport that had replaced the slow Erie Canal boats. Railroads took them across New York to Buffalo, then a steamboat crossed Lake Erie to either Ohio or Michigan. Another train took them to Lake Michigan, where a steamer carried them the rest of the way. The trip was over 1,000 miles.

knew well. Those who made money from the liquor interest were sure to make trouble, but the women were confident they could handle anything that came their way.

After an overnight train trip and a steamboat ride across Lake Michigan, the two reformers docked in Milwaukee. Expecting an enthusiastic welcome from the temperance community, they were instead met by one man who clearly wasn't happy to see them.

The man let them know he was expecting the New York Temperance Society to send a man to speak for temperance. Instead the society had sent not one but *two* women, including a well-known champion of women's rights. He told them that they would disgrace the cause of temperance. They would be jeered by audiences. And he himself would become a laughingstock. On and on he went, Nichols said, "stooping to the most disgusting depths."

Soon the ladies were in for an even ruder shock. The Wisconsin Temperance League had voted to strip them of their responsibilities and withdraw its support. Nichols and Fowler had not reckoned on such a reception in a young pioneer state.

News of the muddle quickly reached the ears of Sherman Booth, the abolitionist editor of Milwaukee's *Daily Free Democrat*. He had shared the platform with Nichols at the recent Whole World's Temperance Convention, which was organized after a similar fiasco in which women were excluded from speaking.

On the pages of his newspaper, Booth related the story of how poorly Nichols and Fowler had been treated. Wisconsin should "joyfully welcome" these women, he wrote. "We believe that no men can be obtained whose services would be half so efficient in this cause."

The state vote on temperance was just five weeks away. "There is no time to be lost," Booth said. "The State must be thoroughly roused."

Nichols and Fowler received a hasty invitation to attend the Wisconsin Women's Temperance Convention in Delavan. Here they were welcomed like heroes. The women at the convention agreed that their state was in crisis and awash in alcohol. They voted not to rest until they had helped reverse the tide. Milwaukee was already something of a hopeless cause. As large numbers of German immigrants poured in, breweries sprang up to serve their national beverage. But the rest of the state was up for grabs.

The Wisconsin Women's Temperance Convention voted to support Nichols and Fowler as they made their own tour of the state. The president of the women's group made a statement on behalf of her society:

"We hereby give notice to the law-makers of Wisconsin, as we have before done, that the Women are COMING: that they are fully determined to give them no peace until they pass a law for suppressing the sale of intoxicating liquors throughout the State."

During October and November of 1853, Nichols and Fowler lectured for four weeks straight without a day's rest. They traveled 900 miles around Wisconsin by horse-drawn wagon or stagecoach. They spoke in 43 towns to more than 30,000 people. In most places standing-room-only crowds gathered to catch a glimpse of them. It was as good a show as the circus. People came in wagons from five to 20 miles to see the amazing attraction — two women lecturing.

Before starting out, Nichols worried that she might not have the stamina to travel and lecture on a daily basis, but the large turnouts, which were generally friendly, both surprised and energized her. Riding through the gently rolling countryside under blue skies in the crisp air of Indian summer, she fell in love with Wisconsin. "Broad prairies, gallant lakes, and noble humanity," she recalled later.

She observed fine brick houses lining the road and men and women hard at work. There were signs of progress everywhere. Even the fences in Wisconsin impressed her; they looked as solid as New England granite.

The biggest challenge on the lecture circuit continued to come from the Temperance League, which had tried to stop the Eastern women's campaign. Now it seemed as eager to discredit the women as to win the anti-liquor vote. Its members would race ahead to the towns Nichols and Fowler were scheduled to lecture in, spreading terrible rumors about the women and warning people to boycott the meetings. Sometimes they would try to get innkeepers to tell the women they had no rooms available.

These efforts backfired. Sympathetic families put them up in their homes. When a minister refused to allow the women to speak in his church, another minister in town would welcome them. Told that they could not address a large church convention in Madison, they were quickly invited to lecture at an even more prestigious location: the chambers of the state assembly.

At a church in Waukesha, the two reformers waited for over an hour while the deacon and another man carried on a long business meeting. It became clear to Nichols that the men's real intention was to keep the women from speaking. Finally, the deacon gathered up his belongings and told everyone to go home.

Cries of protest rose up from the pews. One man said he had come 20 miles on his horse to hear the talk. Another said he had walked 13 miles so that his wife and daughter could ride his horse. Finally, the deacon relented and said the women would be allowed to speak ... on the following night.

What shocked Nichols was that she had recognized the deacon as an old friend from her Brockport days. She had once encouraged him to speak out for temperance at a time when he had been reluctant to do so. Of course, those were different times, when she was Clarina Carpenter and she believed it was improper for a woman to speak in public. She had moved forward — but "my friend," she recalled later, "had only stood still."

When it was her turn to speak the following night, Nichols scanned the audience for the deacon. She spotted him sitting in the middle of the audience. There was no sign that he remembered who she was.

She thanked the congregation for asking her and Mrs. Fowler back. She told them it was not the first time she had been kept from speaking up. Why, there was even a time when an old friend stepped in her path. She and this friend had once been coworkers in the temperance cause in Brockport, and she had supported him, but years later, he would not do the same for her.

Slowly, the deacon's face reddened as he realized that he was the one she was talking about. After the meeting, he came up and apologized. He volunteered to get her an invitation to speak at a county temperance convention. Instead of humiliating her critic, as she had every right to do, Nichols had treated him with compassion and had won back an old ally.

The crusade in Wisconsin was a great success. The temperance law passed, as did another measure that gave wives both control of their property and custody of their children in divorce cases where the husbands were found to be drunkards.

The western trip marked a turn in Nichols' outlook. On the whole, Wisconsin had been good to her. She began to think that men's and women's roles were less rigid in the West than they were in the East. Other than run-ins with male temperance leaders, she found that Westerners were not as tradition-bound as Easterners were. She recalled the sight of wagons heading for the markets in Milwaukee. Atop mountain-high loads of grain were men and tidily dressed women riding side by side.

When she returned from her trip, Clarina found that George's health had worsened. She thought about Wisconsin, its expansive prairies and open-minded people. She began to ponder the idea that the West might help restore George to health — as well as provide new opportunities for her.

A Country Divided

Clarina Nichols returned from Wisconsin on a high note. After a rocky start, her path had been smoothed by new friends. They supported her efforts in their state with great enthusiasm. The entire sequence of events that fall — the raucous conventions in New York, the adventure of traveling to a Western state, and the vigorous campaign that followed — all these boosted her confidence.

In two short years she had changed from a cautious defender of oppressed women to a self-assured advocate of reform. Now she had reached a crossroads. Should she keep the *Democrat* going? Devote herself to lecturing? Move to Wisconsin? George's health had not improved, and her father had become seriously ill. Every week she took the stagecoach from Brattleboro to look in on him and help with his care.

By the end of 1853 she and George decided to close down the *Democrat*. Lecturing would give her more freedom and flexibility than running a weekly newspaper. She felt sure that her growing reputation would result in as many speaking engagements as she desired. She was right.

In late December she lectured in Massachusetts. The following month she was invited to Rhode Island for a four-part series on women's rights. And in March she was booked for two nights at the Tremont Temple in Boston.

Her programs were often set up as debates between all-male and all-female teams. When members of the clergy were present, they were always asked to speak against woman suffrage. Their wives were always assigned to speak in favor of suffrage. It made for a lively evening.

Nichols allowed the ministers to open and close the debate. Even with that advantage, her opponents invariably got the worst of it. Clergymen assumed the lady would be an easy debate opponent. But her understanding of both Scripture and the law surprised and rattled them. Once she got going, the ministers often ended up stammering and apologizing for not being better prepared. After one such debate, a flustered minister said, "I told you, ladies and gentlemen, that I had given little attention to the subject ... and you see that I told the truth."

Nichols was proud of her ability to lay out clear and convincing arguments and to win over skeptics without becoming a "masculine brawler." Still, she was not afraid to throw feminine modesty to the wind when the fate of mothers and children was at stake.

In January 1854 she was riding the train to a speaking event in Templeton, Massachusetts, when she heard a woman crying out in anguish, *"Don't take away my children!"*

Looking up from her knitting, Nichols recognized the two Brattleboro men who were causing the disturbance. One was the village sheriff, the other an older wealthy gentleman from the town.

Nichols set down her needlework and rushed to the mother's side. The passengers craned their necks to see what was happening. All eyes in the train were now riveted upon the dramatic scene — two grown men attempting to grab two small children away from their mother.

Instinctively Nichols knew what to do. Without waiting to hear the details, she addressed the passengers in a loud voice.

"My friends!" she said, "The lawmakers of this Christian country have given the custody of their babies to the fathers, drunken or sober!"

Now the passengers understood what was happening. The sheriff was there to seize the children.

Some passengers began to get out of their seats. Nichols quickly strode over to the door to prevent anyone from leaving. "The excitement was intense," she recalled later. Everyone on the train was on the young mother's side.

The train, which had been parked in the depot, began to pull away. Now the two men in the middle found themselves surrounded with hostile passengers on a train moving rapidly toward the Vermont-Massachusetts state line.

Ever alert to the laws that affected women, Nichols knew that either a father or a grandfather could take children from their mother in Vermont. In Massachusetts, however, only a father had that right. She warned the sheriff that he would soon be in Massachusetts and out of his jurisdiction.

As the train rolled through the countryside, Nichols and her allies worked up a rescue plan. She was not alarmed when the two men hopped off the train at the next stop with the four-year-old in tow. She had enlisted a doctor who was willing to get off the train and escort the mother to local authorities. A man was needed because the law did not allow a woman to file charges on her own.

Nichols volunteered to take the baby with her to the lecture, where she undoubtedly used the child to make several points about what was wrong with the law. She left the baby with a trusted friend who agreed to reunite it with its mother.

Only later did Nichols learn the full story. The mother was suing for divorce, citing domestic abuse. The older gentleman was the woman's father-in-law. He had enlisted the sheriff. The two men had planned to grab the children off the train while it was in the depot and whisk them to a waiting carriage. Her instincts had been exactly right.

A sheriff in Massachusetts tracked down the two men and hauled them into court. They were ordered to return the older child and pay expenses for the trouble they had caused.

News of the dramatic rescue spread quickly. The reports must have included the detail of her knitting, for people sent her skeins of yarn to show approval for what she had done. She gratefully accepted these gifts as evidence that people saw her as she wanted

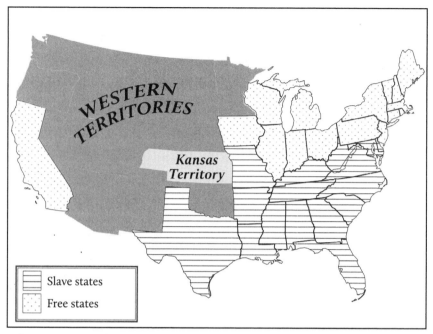

The United States in 1854, when the Kansas-Nebraska Act was passed. With the matter of slavery now put to a vote of the people, the whole country was interested in the direction Kansas would take.

to be seen. She was someone who had "home interests" at heart — someone who was knitting society together instead of unraveling it.

What was tearing the country apart at that moment was debate over the proposed Kansas-Nebraska bill. This bill would open the vast Western territory to white settlers. A provision in the bill called "popular sovereignty" allowed the white men who settled the territories to vote slavery up or down.

The South thought this was a fair way to settle the matter. Nebraska, they reasoned, would enter the Union as a free state, and Kansas — with the help of their neighbors in Missouri — would vote slavery in. Northerners were alarmed. The new bill overturned the 1820 Missouri Compromise that made slavery illegal in Western territories like Kansas and Nebraska. Slavery would be free to would snake its way into the West.

It was a high-stakes situation for both sides. Three thousand New England clergymen sent Congress a petition in opposition to the Kansas-Nebraska bill. They called it "a great moral wrong" that threatened "the peace and even the existence of our beloved union."

Despite fierce opposition by the ministers and other anti-slavery groups, however, the bill became law in May of 1854.

Across New England and in other Northern states, the call went out to flood the territory with settlers who would vote Kansas into the Union as a free state.

Clarina Nichols took a keen interest in this development. Her father died the same month that the Kansas-Nebraska bill passed. In an important way his passing loosened her ties to Vermont. She was free to move on.

The more she learned about Kansas Territory, the more interested she became. For despite her carefully crafted reputation as a genteel voice on behalf of women and children, Nichols had a restless, adventurous spirit that looked outward instead of inward.

Since 1847 she and George had been out of step with their less progressive neighbors. They had broken with the Democratic

Party over the slavery issue. And they were both adamantly opposed to the westward expansion of slavery. Nichols was frustrated by the lack of progress for women in her home state. She was beginning to think she might gain more ground for women in the West than in "conservative old Vermont."

She began meeting with others who were thinking about moving to Kansas Territory. These meetings led to the formation of the New England Emigrant Aid Society. This organization helped hundreds of anti-slavery settlers to emigrate, or move, to Kansas. They traveled in groups and on arrival received help from the society in finding places to live.

That fall Clarina, 20-year-old Howard, and 18-year-old Relie traveled by train to St. Louis, then took a steamboat across the width of Missouri on the river of the same name. At the border with Kansas Territory, they stepped back in time, traveling as their grandparents and great-grandparents had done — by horse and wagon, by oxcart, and on foot.

Clarina left her husband, little George, and Birsha behind. She would return for them if she was convinced that moving to Kansas was the right thing to do. She hoped it would be. In her mind, New England was weighted down by its history. Kansas was a clean slate.

Meat, Mush, Molasses

The fourth party of the New England Emigrant Aid Society departed in October of 1854, more than 200 strong. Clarina counted 30 women and 45 children traveling with her, many more than in previous emigrant groups. She saw this as a good sign, for where women went, homes and civilization followed.

Nichols and her fellow travelers received the kind of patriotic sendoff given to soldiers in the early weeks of a popular war. At the Boston station, crowds of well-wishers joined them in singing the "Hymn of the Kansas Emigrant," written by poet John Greenleaf Whittier:

> We cross the prairies as of old
> The pilgrims crossed the sea,

To make the West, as they the East,
The homestead of the free!

Easterners were fascinated by the Kansas drama. Newspapers could not print enough reports from the site of slavery's showdown in the West. From aboard her Missouri River steamboat, Nichols painted a scene for the readers of the *Boston Evening Telegraph*: "Picture the writer surrounded by some 20 emigrants ... under 6 years of age, who are laughing, crying, tumbling, and being tumbled over." She reported trying to write while overhearing "snatches of song and cheerful, sometimes hilarious, conversation from surrounding groups. Who can think in such a scene?"

The ship's captain asked Nichols to lecture on women's rights during the 10-day journey. She obliged him two nights in a row. Another passenger, whom Nichols described as "a pious doctor," sent his young wife to bed before her talk — obviously so she wouldn't get any new ideas. Knowing where the wife's cabin was located below deck, Nichols stood where the woman could hear, even if she couldn't see.

"Next morning, poor man! His wife was an outspoken advocate of woman's rights," Nichols wrote triumphantly. "The next evening she punched his ribs vigorously at every point made for suffrage, which was the subject of my second lecture."

On a cold and rainy Saturday evening the pioneers docked on the levee in Kansas City, Missouri. What little they could see of the city did not lift their spirits. Rickety houses were perched atop steep hills that overlooked narrow, muddy streets. On the north side of the banks were the wigwams of various Indian tribes that were being displaced by white settlers pushing their way into Kansas.

A band of rough-talking, pro-slavery Missourians decided to serve as the emigrants' welcoming party. They boarded the boat uninvited and proceeded to tell wild tales about savage Indians scalping desperate pioneers. As they carried on, the atmosphere grew increasingly tense. The polite New Englanders were unsure how to respond.

Finally, one of their party introduced himself to Nichols as Colonel Scott. "Can you tell me where all these people are from, and where they are going?" he asked, though he knew perfectly well the answer to his question.

"They are from the New England states and are going to Kansas," she replied, playing along.

The colonel told Nichols that she and her compatriots would never survive pioneer life in Kansas because it was impossible to farm the prairie without slave labor.

Nonsense, Clarina snapped. New Englanders were tough and ingenious. "Did you never hear how in New Hampshire and Vermont the sheep's noses have to be sharpened so that they can pluck the spears of grass from between the rocks?"

The colonel couldn't help laughing at the idea of sharp-nosed sheep plucking grass from the hillside. With that the tension eased. By the time he and his men departed, Colonel Scott had invited Nichols to bring her lecture on women's rights up the river to St. Joseph.

In 1854 Kansas City was a crossroads of East and West. Pio-

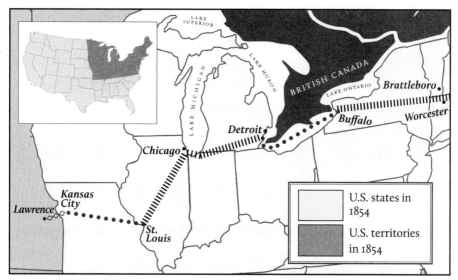

Susan B. Anthony's brother, Daniel Anthony, was with the first New England Emigrant Aid Society group. He kept a journal of the exact route taken to Kansas (shown here). The group took trains and steamboats on their 12–day journey to Kansas City. Then they walked to Lawrence.

neers setting out on the westward trails were outfitting themselves in Kansas City or the nearby towns of Independence and Westport. They bought wagons, ox teams, horses, cattle, saddles, bridles, blankets, camp equipment, flour, coffee, and guns.

The Indians rode in from the territory to trade wares and buy supplies. Trappers and tradesmen swigged home-brewed whisky in public, swore like sailors, and didn't bother looking for a privy when they needed to pee. They carried pistols on their belts and Bowie knives in their boots, and were ready to use both at the slightest provocation. It made for a unpleasant scene, Nichols reported to the Eastern press. "We were all in haste to get away," she added.

When the pioneers crossed the Missouri state line into Kansas Territory, they were overjoyed to find beautiful prairie rolled out as far as the eye could see. To the north stretched a line of forested hills decked out in fall colors familiar to every New Englander. An eagle looking down on the scene would have seen a long, unbroken ribbon of pioneers moving slowly across the prairie on foot, on horseback, and in every kind of rig that could be pulled by horse, mule, or ox.

Emigrants were pouring into Kansas Territory from every direction. Most of the new arrivals were only interested in getting their own piece of cheap land. Some, however, were on a mission for one side or the other. They were intent on seeing that Kansas became either a slave state or a free state.

The fourth Emigrant Aid party, which included Nichols, was bound for the new town of Lawrence. Missourians had already dubbed it "Yankee Town" because of all the New England abolitionists moving there. At the time, Lawrence looked more like a refugee camp than a town. People lived in widely spaced white cotton tents or crude huts with earthen floors. They ate mush and bacon three times a day, often mixed with the ashes scattered by their outdoor fireplaces.

Nichols rode into Lawrence ahead of the others in a covered wagon driven by Colonel Samuel Pomeroy, the guide for her group. As their coach came to a halt, a burst of loud cheering broke out. She soon learned that some of the young men had been arguing about women's rights. When the announcement came that Mrs. Nichols, the famed lecturer from the East, had just arrived, they let out a whoop. As she climbed down from the wagon, the boys begged her to lecture that evening. She turned them down, saying she was exhausted and needed to rest. Someone gave her armloads of prairie hay for a bed and directed her to a central lodging house that had been built for new arrivals.

The next evening, the town dinner bell announced her lecture. The emigrants gathered in their new meeting house — a crude structure made of ridge poles thatched with prairie hay. She stepped up to her podium — two tool boxes stacked on top of each other. As she prepared to speak, she surveyed the novel scene before her. Men and children of all ages rested on bundles of hay strewn about the earthen floor. The women sat on the emigrants' trunks that lined the sides of the meeting house. If any of them got too close to the walls, the hay would tickle their noses. Glass lanterns hung from the ceiling cast a hazy light on the upturned faces of her audience. Everyone looked a little grimy even in soft light, but they were a good audience. An attentive audience. An audience open to new ideas and new voices.

That cool evening in early November of 1854, Clarina Nichols brought the women's rights movement to Kansas Territory. She later wrote that she enjoyed her debut in Kansas "as I have seldom [enjoyed] a lecture."

In the morning she joined other small groups making breakfast on the levee. She watched one middle-aged man try to boil tea and fry sidepork on the same fire without tipping either over. (He didn't succeed.) She noticed with satisfaction that there were as many men cooking their meals as there were women doing so. Nearby, she watched a woman making breakfast, her skirts fringed by prairie stubble and scorched with burn holes. Before

Clarina sketched this view of Lawrence, Kansas, in November 1854.

long, she and other women would be reviving the bloomer craze that had died out in the East.

Nichols saw a group of men standing around a frying pan filled with gravy and bacon. Each man was dipping his bread into the frying pan and plucking out bacon with his fingers. No utensils were required.

In health-conscious Brattleboro, Clarina Nichols had become a vegetarian. In Kansas, however, she was soon eating meat with everyone else. It was one of the few food items that was widely available and affordable. She decided it was a necessary price to pay for being in a new place where there were no markets, gardens, or orchards.

"The climate is the finest," Clarina told her Eastern readers, "and if sickness comes, I shall attribute it to exposure and change of living from a vegetable to a meat diet."

In the days that followed, she borrowed a horse and rode to the top of Mt. Oread, the highest point in Lawrence. From its crest, she could see the countryside spread out like a table before her. She propped herself against a stack of hay and made a pencil sketch of the panorama of woodlands and plateaus surrounding her.

Before her stay came to an end, she helped her sons prepare for winter. They built a sod house from chunks of earth they had cut out of the prairie. And she made a few more observations that she shared with Eastern readers. Men who came west with women fared better than those who came alone, she wrote for the *Springfield* (Mass.) *Daily Republican.* This was because "the women are 'strong-minded,' " she wrote, before quickly assuring readers that this was not an insult. Strong-mindedness was a desirable quality in a pioneer woman.

In December, Nichols returned to Vermont and began packing for a permanent move west. She told old friends that she thought she knew a few things about pioneer life from the stories her grandparents had told her. "But that was all *head* knowledge," she admitted.

Her son Relie gave this advice to the people out East who were thinking of coming to Kansas: "Do not expect to eat oysters or go to a ball the first thing on landing. You must make your arrangements to live on mush and molasses for a week and sleep on a log for a fortnight."

Prairie Home

At the end of November 1854, Kansas Territory held its first election. Hundreds of Missourians streamed across the border to vote. They were defiant, rowdy, liquored up, and well-armed. From a high bluff Nichols watched in astonishment. In Douglas, a town of no more than 50 residents, more than 300 votes were cast. Most were for pro-slavery candidates. The Missourian-backed, pro-slavery ticket swept to an easy victory. The tug of war over the fate of Kansas had begun.

Clarina returned to Vermont to begin preparations to move the rest of her family west. On her way home she passed through Brockport, where by now her work in the women's movement and published reports from Kansas had made her a celebrity. People stopped her on the street to ask her about the latest rumors. Was it true that the territory was overrun with drunken, gun-toting Missourians? (No, she answered, but Kansas City was.) Were the living conditions as primitive as everyone said? (Yes, and then some.)

While in Vermont Nichols gave lectures about the Kansas situation. Her description of pioneer life probably made her former neighbors and friends raise their eyebrows. A reporter covering one of her talks for a local newspaper wrote that he couldn't imagine such a "mixing of the sexes" or such "unhygienic" conditions. If Clarina had read his story she would have laughed.

"Mrs. Nichols is yet hopeful for liberty in Kansas," the reporter at another lecture wrote. He added, though, that the speaker did not provide much proof to support her claim. The reporter pointed out that no free state touched Kansas and that the "slave power" was united, powerful, and "fully awake."

David Rice Atchison, the outspoken senator from Missouri, was telling his fellow Missourians it was their "duty" to ride across the border and vote for slavery in Kansas. With the first election already stolen, it appeared the pro-slavery forces had the advantage.

Winter turned to spring, and Nichols prepared for her family's permanent move to Kansas Territory. By now George was feeling a little better. Howard's fiancée, Sarah Jones, would be joining them. Clarina's 11-year old son George and 23-year-old daughter Birsha would not. They were enrolled in a progressive school in New Jersey run by the Grimké sisters, Sarah and Angelina, who had done much to link women's rights and the anti-slavery cause.

George was planning to join the family in the spring when school let out, while Birsha stayed on in New Jersey. She wrote Clarina, "God only knows what changes time may have wrought in our little circle."

On Clarina's return trip to Kansas with her family, their steamboat kept hitting sandbars in the Missouri River. At one point they were grounded for 18 hours. As the men waded around with long poles prying the boat loose, Nichols delivered a lecture on women's rights to a captive audience.

Once on land, the Nicholses headed for the Baptist mission on the Missouri-Kansas border. The mission had become a popular stopping-off place for new emigrants to Kansas Territory. The day before they arrived, a New Hampshire couple had come to the mission bearing the body of their young son. He had taken sick on the river and died. Unwilling to leave him behind in a slave state, they were bringing his body with them to bury in Kansas Territory.

One night more than 50 people slept at the Baptist mission, bedding down on the main floors, the attic, and the bare ground outside. Mice sometimes nibbled on the sleepers' toes. Most people were so exhausted by their journeys that they barely noticed. Clarina said that if the newcomers still had any starch in their shirts when they arrived in Kansas, it would soon be shaken out.

We do not know what personal items Clarina brought into Kansas Territory. We can get some idea of what was considered essential by reading the list that another pioneer woman prepared for her insurance agency after losing her trunk:

Shawl	$ 8.00	Delaine Dress	9.50
White Basque	3.50	5 Night Dresses	6.50
4 Chemise	6.00	2 Skirts	2.00
3 Pr Drawers	4.50	3 Yds Cotton Cloth	0.38
Thread	.60	1 Brush & 2 Combs	1.50
1 Accordian	2.00	1 Finger Ring	3.00
2 Fine Collars	4.00	1 [Ring]	2.00
1 Pr Mitts	.50	2 Linen Hdkfs	1.00
1 Veil	1.00	1 Rosewood Work Box	3.00
1 Pr Boots	2.50	1 Bible	0.75
1 Pr Ear Rings	2.00	Books	2.00
3 Aprons	.75	3 Daguerrotypes	2.50
Trunk	2.00	4 [items not named]	15.00
1 Wool Plaid Dress	8.00		
2 Calico	3.00	TOTAL	$ 98.73
3 Belt Ribbons	1.25		

Clarina delivered Sarah to Lawrence and she and Howard were promptly married. Clarina then set off in a wagon pulled by a pair of mules. She was heading for the town of Osawatomie to meet up with her husband, who had gone there from Kansas City by another route.

Her driver and guide struck out across the open prairie, "as if such things as surveyed roads were entirely unnecessary," she wrote to readers of a New Hampshire newspaper. The wagon followed the Santa Fe Trail, but only for a couple of miles. Then it crossed two long, lonely stretches of prairie, one 12 miles across, the other eight miles across.

Over hill and valley, through woods and across rivers and creeks, they rattled and bumped along. Some of the ravines were so steep their wagon nearly tipped over. When the exhausted mules could no longer pull the loaded wagon, Clarina hopped out and walked the last 13 miles.

During this trip, she was struck by the "solitude of the prairies." This city girl from the East had a romantic view of country living. In reality Clarina had no experience of rural life beyond occasional visits to someone's farm. Now she found herself in the middle of endless wilderness. In many places there was no sign of human life, no voice except her own and an occasional grunt from her driver. There must have been Indians living here, but they avoided meeting her and did not make themselves visible.

In another month the prairie would be a colorful palette of pink, yellow, blue, and violet wildflowers, but in early April the hills were as brown and barren as camel's humps.

In the spring of 1855 George, Clarina, and her older sons took possession of four claims on Ottawa Creek. "I liked this region of country better than any I have seen," she told her Eastern readers. "Wood and water are abundant and the prairie high and very rich." Neighbors, on the other hand, were "fewer and farther apart than were angels' visits."

From the nearby timber they built a one-room log cabin that could not have been bigger than their parlor back East. Humble though it was, her family was happy to stop camping in tents and have a roof over their heads again. Next in importance was growing their own food. They had brought several weeks' provisions with them, but these were running low. There were no stores, but they were able to buy some supplies from "Tauy" Jones, a wealthy, Eastern-educated Indian farmer who lived on the nearby Ottawa Reserve. Prices were high. A bushel of potatoes cost $3 to $4. Indian meal was upwards of $1.50 per bushel.

George had bargained with the Missourians for a few scrawny head of cattle. He turned them loose on the prairie to fatten up. Clarina's husband was feeling better than he had in a long time. She was pleased to see him making improvements to their claim. But the work was grueling, exhausting, harder than she had ever imagined. She, George, and the two older boys had built their cabin, broke up 40 acres of tough prairie sod, and planted corn, wheat, potatoes, beets, tomatoes, and melons. They did all the work by hand in three short weeks.

She had promised to report back to Eastern newspapers on life in the territory, but by the end of each day she had no energy left for writing. Even so, she managed a few paragraphs, including a colorful description of housekeeping out on the prairie.

Though she had a much smaller home to care for than she did back in Vermont, it was nearly impossible to keep the cabin clean and dry. Dust sifted through the chinks in the logs. During the wet spring everyone tracked in mud so thick it had to be sliced off their boots with a knife. If they left their muddy boots outside, they needed to remember to give the boots a good shaking-out

This 1855 newspaper cartoon of a familiar scene in Kansas Territory was titled, "A Morning Caller."

before putting them on. Rattlesnakes were known to curl up inside shoes, boots, or anything warm.

After the school term was finished, young George joined them in their new home. It was about this time that the editor of the *Kansas Tribune* visited the Nichols claim. "Our dinner was spread upon the lids of three trunks around which we gathered with our benches or stools," he reported. Despite the humble setting, he thought the meal had a simple elegance to it. Afterward, it was time to show the editor the countryside. Clarina climbed onto a large bay horse behind her husband, and the little band rode off across the prairie. It was a lovely, idyllic moment, one of the last the couple would enjoy together.

Fate delivered two cruel blows that first summer. In early June 1855, George Nichols was injured in a farm accident. Then, in August, a hickory rail struck young George, knocking him unconscious and causing his head to swell to an alarming size. To the relief of his anxious mother, her son eventually regained consciousness and was restored to health.

George Senior was not so fortunate. After weeks in bed recovering from his injury, his health declined. Whether it was from a flu-like cold or pneumonia, he teetered for nine days between life and death. At the end of August, he died.

During their 12-year marriage, George Washington Nichols had been a wonderful husband to Clarina and a kind father to all four of her children. He was the only father any of them had ever known. He had taught his wife and her son Relie the newspaper business. He introduced Clarina to politics and encouraged her — as few men of that day would have done — to speak up for what she believed in, and to travel without him. He may have known that someday she would need an independent spirit.

As sad as she was about losing George, she knew she had been fortunate to remarry so well. "I know what a good husband is better than one who has never tried a bad one," she once told Susan B. Anthony.

She snipped a strand of hair from George's head. She had done the same when her father died the year before. George Nichols was buried on the prairie in a grave marked only by a pile of stones.

There was no letup in Clarina's nursing duties that summer. Relie fell ill, as did Howard, who lived nearby with Sarah. Many of the newcomers to Kansas were ill with what was called "ague." The modern name for this malady is malaria, a disease that was common throughout the Midwest. It was likely spread by mosquitoes that came out after a week-long rain in August. Ague could be fatal, but more often the symptoms merely made its victims so miserable they *wished* they were dead. It often recurred after people thought they were rid of it. It could have been worse. In other parts of the territory, the highly contagious and deadly disease of cholera was ravaging the population. At Fort Riley, 50 soldiers died from cholera the same month George Nichols died.

Only after she had nursed her sons back to health did Clarina allow herself to get sick. Nineteen-year-old Relie cared for her "with the tenderness of a woman," she recalled. Yet as difficult as their first year in Kansas had been, the troubles for Clarina's family and their fellow free staters were only beginning.

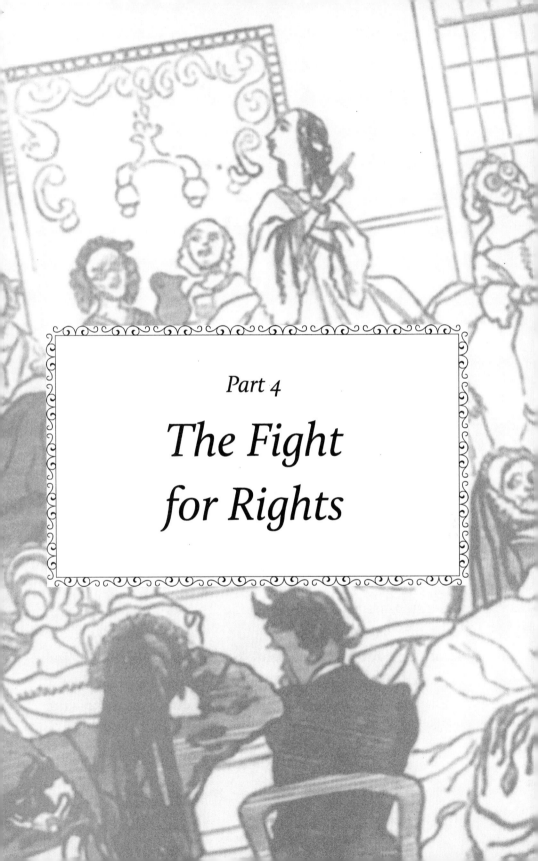

Part 4

The Fight
for Rights

Tinderbox

I n March 1855, the free-state party was once again trounced in elections held in Kansas Territory. Once again Missourians swept across the border the night before, five thousand strong this time. They not only cast votes for slavery in Kansas. They kept the free-state men from voting by beatings and threats of lynching.

Tensions built throughout Kansas Territory. The pro-slavery legislature laid down the law, hard. Writing and speaking out against slavery became criminal offenses punishable by fines and imprisonment. Aiding fugitive slaves became a capital offense, one that could result in hanging. It was even a crime to write newspaper articles condemning slavery.

The free-state men responded by holding their own elec-

THE DAY OF
OUR ENSLAVEMENT!!

To-day, Sept. 15, 1855, is the day on which the ini-

quitous enactment of an illegitimate, illegal and fraudulent Legislature have declared commences the prostration of the Right of Speech and the curtailment of the **LIBERTY OF THE PRESS**!! To-day commences an Era in Kansas which, unless the sturdy voice of the People, backed, if necessary, by "strong arms and the sure eye," shall teach the tyrants who attempt to enthrall us the lesson which our Fathers taught to kingly tyrants of old, shall prostrate us in the dust, and make us the slaves of an Oligarchy.

Worse than the veriest Despotism on Earth!

To-day commences the operation of a law which declares; "Sec. 12. If any free person, by speaking or by writing, assert or maintain that persons have not the right to hold slaves in this Territory, or shall introduce into this Territory, print, publish, write, circulate or cause to be introduced into this Territory, written, printed, published or circulated in this Territory, any book, paper, magazine, pamphlet or circular, containing any denial of the right of persons to hold slaves in this Territory, such person shall be deemed guilty of Felony, and punished by imprisonment at hard labor for a term of not less than two years."

Now we DO ASSERT and we declare, despite all the

bolts and bars of the iniquitous Legislature of Kansas, that

"PERSONS HAVE NOT THE
RIGHT TO HOLD SLAVES IN THIS
TERRITORY."

And we will emblazon it upon our banner in letters so large and in language so plain that the infatuated invaders who elected the Kansas Legislature, as well as

THAT CORRUPT AND IGNORANT LEGISLATURE

Itself, may understand it — so that, if they cannot read,

they may SPELL IT OUT, and meditate and deliberate upon it; and we hold that the man who fails to utter this self evident truth, on account of the insolent enactment alluded to, is a poltroon and a slave worse than the black slaves of our persecutors and oppressors,

The Constitution of the United States, the great Magna Charta of American Liberties,

Guarantees to every Citizen the Liberty of Speech and
the Freedom of the Press!

And this is the first time in the history of Amer. that a body claiming Legislative powers has dared to attempt to wrest these from the people. And it is not only the right, but the bounden duty of every Freeman to spurn with contempt and trample under foot an enactment which thus basely violates the rights of Freemen. For our part we DO and SHALL CONTINUE to utter this truth so long as we have the power of utterance, and nothing but the brute force of an overbearing tyranny can prevent us.

Will any citizen — any free American — brook the insult of

AN INSOLENT GAG LAW!!

The work of a Legislature elected by bullying ruffians who invaded Kansas with arms, and whose drunken revelry, and insults to our peaceable, unoffending and comparatively unarmed citizens, were a disgrace to manhood, and a burlesque upon popular Republican Government! If they do, they are slaves already, and with them Freedom is but a mockery.

After the pro-slavery legislature passed a law prohibiting anti-slavery views from being published in Kansas Territory, a free-state printer let everyone know exactly what he thought of the "gag law."

tion, writing a constitution, and forming a legislature in Topeka. Throughout 1855 and 1856 there were two governments in Kansas. Each claimed to be the legitimate ruling body for the territory.

The two sides eyed each other warily. Taunts, threats, and fist-fights occurred when they crossed paths. A minister who bravely (or foolishly) preached abolition in the pro-slavery town of Atchison was beaten by a mob, tied to a raft, and set adrift in the Missouri River. A free-state man was murdered over a claim dispute. An abolitionist was killed in Lawrence.

In October 1855 a man arrived in the territory who began keeping score of the wrongs committed against anti-slavery settlers. John Brown was in Kansas for one purpose: to see that it never became a slave state. He arrived and joined his sons, who like everyone else had fallen ill from the ague and were unprepared for the winter ahead. By contrast, their father was hale and hearty and unshakable in his belief that slavery was a great sin against the Creator. John Brown had come heavily armed, prepared to wage war against the pro-slavery interests in Kansas.

The territory was a tinderbox waiting for the spark that would ignite it. Both sides bolted their doors at night, stockpiled weapons, and talked anxiously about what they would do if attacked.

Clarina and her boys were no exception. "Sharps rifles are in all our cabins," she wrote in the *New Hampshire Sentinel* the month Brown arrived. Arms, particularly Sharps rifles, were flowing into Kansas, sometimes in boxes marked "Bibles" or "Dry Goods." Nichols once considered herself a pacifist, opposed to all forms of war. A few short months in the territory had changed her mind, almost as quickly as it had changed her mind on eating meat.

In December pro-slavery forces lay siege for a week to Lawrence. Nichols' older sons rode over to join the free staters. She recalled one anxious night during the siege sitting in her cabin far from any neighbors or towns. While her youngest boy slept peacefully in his bed, she worried about her older boys' safety. As she waited in the "fearful silence" for the sounds of approaching Missourians, the silence was suddenly broken by the hoot of an owl, then a chorus of owls. It was so unexpected that she burst out laughing.

With winter approaching, Nichols prepared to return to Vermont to close her husband's small estate. The Missouri River was already impassable by steamboat because of the ice, but she convinced the mail carrier to take her in his stagecoach. He advised her to take the Vermont labels off her baggage.

The Missourians she met along the way surprised her with their gallantry and hospitality. Whenever her stagecoach got stuck in the mud or snow, she would hop out, walk to the nearest cabin, and knock on the door. The men inside would go out to help free the carriage, while she stayed inside and sat by the fire. No matter what the hour or how humble the dwelling, she was always warmly welcomed.

In the gray dawn one morning she roused a family of eight from sleep. They had been living in a windowless cabin with an open doorway for the past four years. She asked the man of the house about the missing door.

"I hung it there," said the Missourian, "but my wife thought it was in the way — and I took it down again!"

Bleeding Kansas

On Christmas Day 1855 it was minus 30 degrees and snowing in Kansas Territory. The pioneers gave up trying to stay warm and concentrated on not freezing to death. They strung sheets above their beds to keep the snow that sifted through the cracks from falling on them as they slept. Water hauled in from the creek froze into solid blocks of ice by midnight and had to be thawed to make coffee in the morning. Frigid winds whipped through the walls of the settlers' flimsy cabins as wolves howled in the timberlands.

Clarina was back in Brattleboro, settling George's estate. After his debts were paid, his daughters given their inheritance, and the lawyers' fees deducted, Clarina received $200. From her father's estate the previous year she received around $1,400. Over the course of her life she would inherit several thousand dollars more from her father's and mother's estates. This was enough to help her through some of the hard times, but not enough to make her a wealthy woman.

As a lasting memento to the two most important men in her life, Clarina took the strands of white and brown hair she had clipped from her father's and her husband's heads and wove them into a brooch, an ornamental pin. Many Victorian women, including Queen Victoria herself, memorialized their loved ones in this way, twisting the hair into pins, bracelets, or even large wreaths. The brooch's special meaning was not lost on the descendants of Clarina Nichols. They have preserved the keepsake to this day.

Widows were normally expected to wear black and be in mourning for their departed loved ones for up to a year before returning to an active social life. But events in Kansas were about to pull Nichols back into the fray. The free-state men were organizing their rival government out of Topeka, and the federal government — which backed the pro-slavery side — was taking notice.

In January of 1856 President Franklin Pierce sent a message to Congress. In it he branded the free-state men as traitors and revolutionaries. He ordered all Kansans to recognize the pro-slavery legislature as the ruling power or face imprisonment. The free-state men snubbed the President and vowed to keep up the fight against the pro-slavery government, which they called the "bogus" legislature.

But the situation was more complicated than that. The fight in Kansas was not simply between the good guys who wanted to end slavery and the bad guys who wanted to extend it.

Many free-state men who were opposed to slavery did not oppose it on moral grounds. They were opposed to slavery because they believed it gave slave owners unfair economic advantages. Slave owners could sell their goods more cheaply than could men who had to pay for labor. These anti-slavery settlers wanted Kansas to be an all-white state.

Not Clarina. She opposed slavery on moral grounds and opposed making Kansas an all-white state. As the free staters argued among themselves, she feared that the "old prejudices" would drown out more progressive voices.

"The black male and the white females," she asked, "what will [the free-state men] do for them?"

In the summer of 1855, she decided to give the anti-black and anti-women's rights men a piece of her mind. For this purpose she hauled in Deborah Van Winkle and let her speak up. The salty Vermonter made an appearance in the Lawrence, Kansas, abolitionist weekly, the *Herald of Freedom*.

"Nobody out here knows anything about *women's* rights," Mrs. Van Winkle complained in a letter to the newspaper. "*Our* rights will never be won and secured while slavery tramples upon our black sisters."

That got a quick reply from another letter-writer, who went under the pen name of Back Woodsman. He identified himself as a white free-state man from Missouri who had come to Kansas because he was tired of living under the "tyrannies and oppressions of slavery." The Back Woodsman said that most free-state men didn't want anything to do with black men or women, slave

Eastern newspaper cartoonist's depiction of Missourians illegally voting in Kansas Territory in 1855.

or free. He advised Mrs. Van Winkle to calm down, because "when we all get to Heaven we'll be white," so let's "stop quarrelin'" and "make Kansas a free white State."

Nichols knew there were a lot of racist free-state men like the Back Woodsman. It would be an uphill battle to change their minds about living and working alongside blacks in Kansas. At least the free staters could all agree on not allowing slavery to move into the West.

At that time the political situation in Kansas was still very fluid. No one could have predicted whose ideas would win the day. Clarina was determined to be heard, to get her beliefs into the mix and to continue pushing for the rights of women, black and white.

Though still out East, she mailed a series of articles on women's rights to the *Herald of Freedom*, which began printing them in the spring of 1856. Nichols reminded her readers that their forefathers had fought a bloody revolution to gain their rights. Then they had turned around and denied women and many other Americans those very same rights. Like Abigail Adams, who had urged her husband John Adams to "remember the ladies" when writing the U.S. Constitution, Nichols planned to make sure the free-state men remembered the ladies when they wrote the constitution for Kansas.

First, though, the free-state cause had to win. The chance of that happening seemed to be going from bad to worse. A pro-slavery judge rounded up the free-state leaders in the territory. Nichols' friend and ally, Charles Robinson, the abolitionist leader of the free staters, was accused of treason and imprisoned.

Then in May, Senator Charles Sumner of Massachusetts was beaten to within an inch of his life on the floor of the Senate in Washington, D.C. His attacker was a Southern congressman who was outraged by Sumner's speech against slavery. Most Northerners were horrified by the attack. Most Southerners thought Sumner had gotten what he deserved.

The very next day — May 21, 1856 — pro-slavery forces launched their largest attack yet on the free-state stronghold of Lawrence. They destroyed the Free-State Hotel with cannon fire, burned many buildings, and dumped the presses of the *Herald of Freedom* into the Kansas River. The last article in Clarina's series on women's rights went down with the presses to the bottom of the river. According to her, this was the article where she made the case for woman suffrage.

Outnumbered, the free-state men stood back and watched as the pro-slavery forces ransacked the town. By the time John Brown and his sons arrived on the scene, much of the city was destroyed or in smoking ruins.

Nichols had received news at a friend's house in New York of both attacks. "The late news from Kansas and the horrible outrage on Senator Sumner in Congress have roused me from the stupor of my grief," she wrote a friend, "and I feel an intense desire to be up and doing." It seemed to her that "only when an evil becomes intolerable do men or states rouse themselves to eradicate it."

Many abolitionists felt the same way as Nichols. But none felt more passionately about the need to "eradicate" the evil of slavery than John Brown.

As angry as Brown and his sons were by the attacks on Sumner and Lawrence, they were even more incensed by the lack of action on the part of the free-state men. The Browns found it outrageous that no resistance had been offered to the Missourians. A combination of rage and frustration boiled up, making the Browns, in one observer's description, "crazy — *crazy!*" Within hours of the attack on Lawrence, John Brown had decided to take matters into his own hands.

Under cover of darkness a group of men — several of the Browns and their accomplices — approached three cabins in the

John Brown in a photograph from the 1850s. An unsuccessful farmer from New York with a large family, Brown believed passionately that slavery was a moral evil.

remote wooded areas along Pottawatomie Creek. They called five men from their cabins and executed them, slashing their throats and hacking off fingers and arms with broad swords. All the murdered men were pro-slavery settlers, but none owned slaves. Two of the victims were brothers, barely out of their teens.

Federal troops were sent to capture the suspected killers. John Brown quickly recruited about 30 of his free-state neighbors and formed a militia. Many of these men found it hard to believe that Old Brown could murder five men in cold blood. Others — including Clarina's two sons, Relie and Howard Carpenter — signed up for the militia because they believed John Brown was fighting for a righteous cause.

On a stretch of prairie known as Black Jack, near Baldwin City, the Federals caught up to Brown's militia. And here, many people argue, is where the Civil War began. The Battle of Black Jack on June 2, 1856, wasn't very big, and it wasn't very bloody. But it was the first military battle between pro-slavery and anti-slavery forces in American history.

Remarkably, Brown's little army carried out several cagey maneuvers and surrounded the small band of Federals, forcing them to surrender. It was a stunning victory and gave the free staters a dose of confidence about the future of their cause.

Clarina's son Relie, however, had caught a bullet in the shoulder during the battle. It was a serious wound that would take weeks of recovery. Most of that time he would spend at a nearby house belonging to an Irish immigrant family, the McCowens. He sent the bullet, which he said had grazed his heart, to his anxious mother in Vermont. She used it as a visual aid in her lectures on Kansas.

"My son lives to fight another day in the hand-to-hand struggle against the most monstrous oppression that the civilized world has ever seen," she declared. "I thank Heaven that I have sons ready to live or die for the rights for which their great-grandfathers fought."

Nichols considered going back to Kansas to be with her family and fellow free-state emigrants. But 1856 was an election year, and she decided she would be of more use by staying out East and working for John C. Frémont. He was a dashing adventurer, an abolitionist, a supporter of women's rights, and the nominee of the country's newest political party, the Republicans. "Frémont and Free Kansas!" was their rallying cry.

The Republicans had plenty of support in New England and New York, but if Frémont was to be elected, the party would need to carry Pennsylvania. That was going to be difficult, because that state was home to the Democratic candidate, James Buchanan.

So Clarina Nichols went to Pennsylvania. That summer she gave 50 lectures throughout the Keystone State. Because of her first-hand knowledge of the situation in Kansas, and because she was one of the country's first-ever female political stump speakers, she was a popular draw. Her calendar quickly filled with speaking engagements. Most of the time her audiences received a triple dip: a lecture on free-state Kansas, a lecture on candidate Frémont, *and* a lecture on women's rights. For her talks she earned $50 a week after expenses, which she sent to her sons fighting in what she called "the Free State Army of Kansas."

She described a desperate situation among the settlers that was meant to shock her listeners. Some of the women, she said, were "so poorly clad that they are ashamed to be seen by strangers. Many of them have cut up their undergarments to make pantaloons for the men."

Her allies in the women's rights movement pledged their support. "Poor bleeding Kansas — how the soul sickens," Susan B. Anthony wrote her in September. "All free State men & women will be crushed out, ere [before] the North will awake."

Near the end of October, Nichols made her way to New York City. Leaders of the National Kansas Committee were holding a big rally in lower Manhattan and wanted her on hand to share her perspective and to plead for aid. Rallies like this were being held across the North on behalf of "bleeding Kansas."

Women who belonged to various types of ladies' aid societies pledged their energies to Kansas instead of overseas missions. They held clothing drives and quilting bees. They sponsored bake sales and ice cream socials. They sold flowers and fruits. The money was donated to the National Kansas Committee.

Nichols' job was to identify leaders in each community who would continue to work for Kansas after she left. Most of all, her job was to inspire these women to work hard for the cause of freedom.

"Are you mothers?" she would ask her audiences. "Let me speak to you for the mothers of Kansas. I am one of them. My sons are among the sufferers and defenders of that ill-fated territory. Their blood has baptized the soil which they yet live to weep over, to love, and to defend."

She wasn't above salting her speeches with a little guilt. "Don't ever tell me 'your Eastern friends sympathize with you in your noble struggle for liberty.' Such friends, if one were hanging to a rope for dear life, would look over from the ship's side and cry, 'my sympathies are with you — hang on till you drown!' "

Nichols skipped that fall's Seventh National Woman's Rights Convention. Though she was still in the East, she seems to have been too consumed with politics and her lectures to travel to New York City.

There was another factor at work. Clarina Nichols was becoming a Westerner, or at least a hybrid of Easterner and Westerner. She lived in a very different world than the one she had once inhabited. Her experiences set her apart from her Eastern sisters. She longed at times to live near women "whose whole souls were in the movement instead of unused scraps of heart." It is clear, however, that she found satisfaction in her new life, despite its hardships. She had come to prefer it over life in the East. Though she spent more than a year outside Kansas Territory, there was never any doubt that she would return.

By 1856 the national women's rights movement had come of age. Those involved in it now had a common history, and they recalled it like old soldiers telling war stories at a reunion. The convention's president, Lucy Stone, gave an address listing all the gains that had been made in the past year. From Michigan to Maine, Illinois to New Hampshire, the movement had seen encouraging changes made in property and custody laws for women.

"And Wisconsin — God bless these young states! — has granted almost all that has been asked except the right of suffrage," Stone said. She told the delegates that suffrage would not be long in coming.

Quindaro

When Clarina returned to Kansas Territory in the spring of 1857, the worst appeared to be over. A new governor had quieted down the region. President Pierce had made good on his promise and sent in federal troops to break up the free-state legislature in Topeka. But by that time the momentum was clearly shifting away from the pro-slavery forces. There were just too few of them and too many free staters moving in.

Nichols had promised her Eastern donors that she would give them a report on how the supplies they had sent to Kansas Territory were holding up. Everywhere she went she saw people drinking "charity tea" and "charity coffee" sweetened by "charity sugar." Kansans were making good use of other donations as well.

Birsha (in back), Relie (left), and Howard Carpenter, in a photo from the 1850s.

In many places it looked like people had just reached into the donated barrels of clothing and put on whatever they pulled out. The emigrants weren't fussy about what they wore.

When their skirts started to look ragged, the women turned them inside out — or upside down — and wore them that way a while. Housewives cut the legs off trousers, gave the legs a quarter turn, and sewed them back on again before the knees wore through. They repaired cuffs, replaced collars, and patched holes with whatever scrap of fabric was at hand. Their patchwork sometimes looked comical, but their thriftiness and "good housewifery" warmed Nichols' heart. So did the sight of women wearing men's pants or fashioning their own bloomers.

During the time her son Relie spent recuperating at the McCowen cabin, he had gotten to know the family well — especially their pretty 18-year-old daughter Helen. On Christmas Day, 1856, they married.

Upon his mother's return, Relie informed her that he, Helen, and the McCowens were done with Kansas. It was too much the wild West for them. The family had lost their livestock in a raid by the Missourians. And "the violent thunderstorms are enough to wreck the nerves of Hercules," wrote Helen in her journal. Also, "the rattlesnakes are as thick as the leaves of the trees." After a little more than a year in the territory, Helen had decided "I can bid Kansas goodbye without a regret." They were pushing off for California.

Late that spring five wagons, their white tops gleaming in the sun, began rolling westward across the green grass prairie. On a bright red seat in the middle wagon rode Relie and Helen, side by side, just like the pioneer couples Clarina had observed in Wisconsin.

She must have been sad to see them go. Relie was the child most like her — intelligent and thoughtful, but restless and ambitious too. She still had her other three children nearby. Young George lived with her along with Birsha, who had rejoined the family. Howard and his wife Sarah had a new baby and were eager to settle down near the others.

Truth be told, Clarina was ready for a change of scenery herself. She missed the closeness of neighbors and wanted to be part of town life again. Quindaro gave her that chance.

Defiantly perched on the banks of the Missouri River, the town of Quindaro sprang up in 1857 in response to a need for supplies. Pro-slavery forces had blockaded every port along the Missouri, so the free-state men needed to build a port of their own. They sent out a surveying team. Just north of the juncture of the Missouri and Kansas Rivers, they found a natural rock harbor. Above it they began building a new settlement.

Wyandot Indians held claim to the land, but they welcomed the free-state settlers. They proposed naming the town after a respected Wyandot woman, Quindaro Brown Guthrie. In the Wyandot language *Quindaro* meant simply "a bundle of sticks." The free staters creatively interpreted this to mean "in unity there is strength."

When Nichols arrived, the town of Quindaro was taking shape at a rapid pace. Bushes, small trees, and undergrowth had been cleared out and burned on several acres of bottomland. In the clearing, she reported to a local newspaper, "a hundred buildings — many of them of stone and brick — including hotels, Dry Goods, Hardware, and Grocery stores, a Church and School house, had been built." Making all of this possible was a huge sawmill the settlers had erected, said to be one of the largest in the territory. The new residents quickly caught a case of boom town fever, telling outsiders that *Quindaro will be the greatest city west of Chicago!*

While all the racket was filling the town with noise — banging, hammering, and sawing — another project was quietly taking place out of public view. When word came that a fugitive slave needed help, certain people in Quindaro were alerted. Staying in the shadows, keeping one eye open for those who couldn't be trusted, these abolitionists hid slaves, supplied them with food and clothing, and transported them to the next safe house.

All three races — Indian, black, and white — cooperated in the work of this secret network sometimes called "the underground railroad." Quindaro was ideally located. It lay directly across the river from Parkville, Missouri, an area with a large slave population. Freedom lay within reach if that river could just be crossed, a task made easier during the winter of 1857–58 when the Missouri froze over.

One night two men ran away from a plantation near Parkville, one still dragging his chains behind him. They took a canoe across the river and hid in the brush at the foot of the bluff. There they made contact with some young free-state men who happened to be living at the safe house that underground railroad agents in Quindaro had nicknamed "Uncle Tom's Cabin."

After the manacles were filed off the one man's ankles, the fugitives hid themselves inside wooden crates marked "Dry Goods" and were sent off to Lawrence. On a lecture tour out East the following year, Nichols brought along the broken shackles so her audiences could feel the weight of slavery for themselves.

Quindaro posed a number of physical challenges to the bounty hunter looking for fugitives. The terrain rose sharply from the Missouri River into rocky bluffs and steep hills with deep ravines and valleys cutting across them. Much of the area was heavily wooded but opened into a high meadow. This allowed keen-eyed lookouts to spot hostile visitors approaching in time to alert the townsfolk.

"Of the many slaves who took the train of freedom there," Nichols recalled, "only one — and he through lack of caution in his approach for help — was ever taken back to Missouri."

Caroline

One evening around dusk, a neighbor came to Clarina's house in Quindaro with a young fugitive named Caroline. Her little daughter had been wrenched from her earlier that day and sold to a slave trader heading to Texas. During the violent struggle and escape, Caroline's arm had been broken. Now she was at this white woman's house, asking for a place to hide from men who were trying to capture her.

Fussy housekeeper that she was, Nichols had just scrubbed out her cistern that very morning. It was clean and dry and a perfect place, she thought, for Caroline to hide. The injured woman gingerly climbed down a ladder into the deep hole. Clarina handed down a chair, pillow, and blanket to make Caroline as comfortable as possible for what could wind up being a long wait. Then she covered the cistern with a lid. She placed a wash tub and other supplies nearby so it would look like the cistern was full of water.

Thirteen-year-old George had a part to play as well. His mother set up a cot with a basin and medicines nearby. If any of the men searching for Caroline would come to their house, George would pretend to be ill, and Clarina would pretend to be caring for him. Not only would it provide an alibi in the middle of the night — for Clarina would be unable to sleep while guarding her fugitive — but the threat of catching the ague would probably encourage the bounty hunter to move along.

Word got back to the Nichols house that Quindaro was hot with slave hunters. Fourteen of them had fanned out across town, all of them searching for one young black woman. They searched the town and the surrounding countryside. It seemed like they would never leave.

"All night I crept to and fro in slippered feet, whispering words of cheer to Caroline in her cell," Nichols recalled. As anxious as she felt, her charge must have been exhausted, overcome with fear, despondent over the loss of her child — but perhaps hopeful that a better life was ahead for her in Canada. Nichols would certainly have been thinking back to the day when Justin had taken their children away from her and vanished. Caroline would not be as lucky as she had been, for it was unlikely she would ever see her daughter again.

The next morning, 14 slave hunters rode away empty-handed. The railroad agents waited through the day until they could make a move. Caroline sweated a few more hours in the dark cistern.

Without the brave actions of thousands of fugitive slaves, there never would have been an underground railroad. This 1862 painting by the artist Eastman Johnson depicts a family in the Civil War dashing to freedom behind Union Army lines.

Finally that evening, she and another young fugitive mother climbed into the back of a wagon, hidden behind merchandise, and were taken north to Leavenworth, the next stop on their bittersweet journey to Canada and freedom.

Even the free African Americans living in Kansas Territory had to watch themselves. Nichols warned her fellow settlers of the "Missouri wretches" who had kidnapped a free black woman she had hired to keep house for the family when she was away on business. The woman's husband was able to get her back, but

Nichols knew that such outcomes were rare.

When it came to the underground railroad, Nichols had to be cautious about what she said in public. One detail let slip to the wrong person could endanger the lives of a whole chain of fugitives or those helping them. Even her letters had to disguise any mention of the underground railroad. She wrote a friend that some "blessed events" had recently occurred in Quindaro. She did not say what those events were but wrote, "Humanity can have railroads without grants from Congress." Her friend would have known immediately that Nichols was not talking about the transcontinental railroad that would soon run through Kansas. The underground railroad was "Humanity's railroad." The "blessed events" were the successful escapes of slaves on the "train" to freedom that regularly pulled out of the Quindaro "station."

Hunting human beings as if they were animals outraged Nichols. She spotted a handbill posted in town offering $500 for the return, "dead or alive," of an enslaved young man who had liberated himself and was making a run to freedom. The reward disgusted her and as soon as she got home, she took out her portable writing desk and began composing lines:

> *To the hunt! To the hunt!*
> *Take bloodhound and gun —*
> *The quarry is noble —*
> *A chattel [slave] has run.*

She finished the poem and mailed it in to the *Lawrence Republican,* which printed it.

Birsha Carpenter had been hired to teach in the new Quindaro schoolhouse. Her mother helped her at the school. Both women insisted that classes be open to black children, white children, and Indian children alike. This turned out to be an unpopular policy, even among the supposedly progressive citizens of Quindaro. One neighbor told Clarina that she and Birsha would soon be "starving," just so they could teach a few black and Indian students. She replied curtly, "We will wait until we *have* starved before we abandon them."

But the neighbor had a point. Nichols later estimated that their school would have enrolled at least three times the number of tuition-paying students if they had simply excluded blacks.

And there were other discouraging trends around town. She seems not to have found a home among the churches that sprang up around Quindaro. Even in the West most congregations were run by ministers who commanded women to be silent, to submit to their husbands, and to resist the evil doctrine of suffrage.

Instead, Nichols wrote about the comfort and inspiration she found in nature and from taking long rambles through the woods. She complained about the developers who were clearing acres of trees outside Quindaro. In the local paper, the *Chindowan*, she urged others to enjoy the natural surroundings while they could. "Go to the grand old woods, sisters," she wrote, "before the woodsman fells the trees and works the ruin of beauty which it has taken ages to perfect."

The *Chindowan* would have been a fine newspaper to associate with, and for a time Nichols did, even earning a spot on the masthead. Alas, the editor, J.M. Walden, was more interested in her writings about education, gardening, the joys of motherhood and clean laundry, the virtues of paid labor (as opposed to slave labor), the Wyandot lands, and of course, temperance. But Walden was opposed to women's rights, and resisted efforts by Nichols to publish her pieces on suffrage. Finally, she asked that her name be removed from the masthead of the *Chindowan*.

On a brighter note, the political tide was finally starting to turn in Kansas Territory. Free staters were coming in not only on the Missouri River, but on the overland Lane Trail across Iowa. By the fall of 1857, it was plain to see that they greatly outnumbered the men who favored slavery.

The October general election confirmed it. Free-state men went to the polls and won an overwhelming victory. Their party gained control of both houses in the territorial legislature. Nichols wrote to a Vermont newspaper that Kansas was about to see the "dawn of freedom on her glorious prairies."

President Buchanan — a Democrat who was every bit the supporter of Southern rights that President Pierce had been — led a final desperate attempt to bring Kansas into the Union as a slave state. A pro-slavery constitution was drafted in the territorial capital at Lecompton and submitted to Congress. But it failed narrowly.

Violence between pro- and anti-slavery settlers continued to flare up, and a massacre near Marais des Cygnes River in 1858 made headlines from coast to coast. For the most part, though, bloodshed gave way to good old-fashioned bickering, as rival politicians struggled for control of the Free State Party.

By the time the ports up and down the Missouri River began opening up to free-state traffic, many in Quindaro had grown weary of living in a remote village near a steep cliff and a hard-to-access port. They began moving to less rugged townsites. Quindaro began to empty out.

Nichols, though, would keep her home there through the Civil War, until 1868, when Quindaro was practically a ghost town. She may have held on in the hope that one day she could make back her investment. But she always had more than a monetary interest in Quindaro. She loved its beautiful placement on the high bluff, and more importantly, she loved what it had stood for.

"Many a brave deed was done there," she would recall, "and many a mean one circumvented, of which the world outside knew nought."

Wyandotte

A convention was planned for the summer of 1859 to draft yet another constitution for the would-be state of Kansas. With the free-state forces firmly in control of the territory, the delegates who gathered in Wyandotte City in July 1859 knew that they were likely determining the laws that all Kansans would eventually abide by. Various groups of men had created three earlier constitutions that failed to be adopted for one reason or another.

The Topeka Constitution of 1855 had outlawed slavery, but it also prohibited African Americans from living or working in the state. There was the notorious Lecompton Constitution, which had come close to passing Congress in 1858 and would have admitted Kansas to the Union as a slave state. A third constitution, drafted in Leavenworth in 1858, probably in reaction to Lecompton, outlawed slavery and gave black males the right to vote. Within Kansas Territory there were sentiments for all three points of view.

Nichols had thought long and hard about this moment. This would be her best chance to insert women's rights into a state constitution. She decided on a petition drive. Her goal would be to deliver as many signatures as possible, male and female, to the organizers of the convention. The petition would demand that the delegates include no rights in the constitution that could be denied on the basis of sex.

Later, she wrote that she had thought about using the phrase "sex or race" in her petition. Given the racism of many free-state men, however, she decided that the inclusive language would "do no good" for either blacks or women. Nichols felt sure that if women got the ballot, they would elect men who would in turn vote for black suffrage.

She got some unexpected help from other settlers. In Linn County, a good day's ride from Quindaro, two sisters-in-law, Susan and Esther Wattles, had formed the Moneka Women's Rights Association along with Esther's husband John and more than 40 others. The Wattles women were bloomer-wearing abolitionist Quakers who wanted to see the higher-paying professions, like law and medicine, opened to women. Two of Susan's daughters would later become physicians, and Esther's three daughters all did advanced studies at Oberlin College in Ohio.

The women's rights supporters in Moneka soon learned about the Nichols petition drive and were excited to sign up. Susan

Wattles wrote Clarina to announce that "with great pleasure shall we look to you to take the lead in this movement."

Nichols wrote back that Susan's words had given her confidence about presenting her demands in person to the delegates in Wyandotte. "To feel perfectly in place I want to be authorized by petitioners — by my own sex especially," she wrote. She had secured funding for her petition drive from the wealthy abolitionist Wendell Phillips, who had led her to the podium at the Second National Women's Rights Convention just eight short years ago. How much had changed since then.

Collecting signatures in Kansas Territory was no simple matter. There were no trains, and roads were often little more than trails. In bad weather they were impassable. That spring of 1859, the creeks and rivers had overflowed their banks. Swift currents and driftwood made fording rivers dangerous, and there was no getting away from the mud. One observer said that Kansas mud was as slippery as grease and as sticky as tar.

After the flooding subsided, everyone went into the fields to put in the crops that had been delayed. There were no extra horses or rigs to hire, and every able-bodied man was in the fields. "There is no man to go with me and I don't want one," Nichols wrote to Susan B. Anthony. She was confident that she could navigate the roads and handle a petition drive all by herself. "I am in perfect trim physically," she declared, "which is what I never was [back] East."

She decided to visit only the largest settlements in the territory and speak at meetings hosted by local residents who were sympathetic to her cause. To these men and women she would give copies of the petition and urge them to get as many signatures as possible — especially those of women. In this way she collected almost six hundred signatures, an impressive total for a supposedly unpopular cause in a sparsely populated territory.

In July she borrowed a pony from her neighbor Quindaro Brown Guthrie and rode the five miles to the convention in Wyandotte City. She stepped into the large, unplastered hall — located under a second-floor saloon — and presented her stack of petitions to the presiding officer.

As a backup plan, in case the signatures did not gain her entry to the proceedings, she asked for a press pass. As it turned out, she wouldn't need one.

The 52 delegates were gathered in a room with just three windows in front and three windows in back. As the day wore on, the temperature outside climbed over the 100-degree mark and stayed there, turning the convention hall into an oven. An early observer of Kansas made up this humorous "forecast" of a typical summer week in the territory:

> *Day 1 — hot.*
> *Day 2 — hotter.*
> *Day 3 — hottest.*
> *Day 4 — hottentot.*
> *Day 5 — hottentissimo!*

The air inside the convention hall was not only stifling hot but

The state of politics in Kansas Territory was nicely captured by this cartoon from 1858 titled, "A Peace Convention at Fort Scott."

foul-smelling, for many of the men smoked or chewed tobacco. They spat the sickly-sweet juice on the floor, which was the custom when spittoons were not provided.

And though the room was composed mostly of free-state men, they were hardly united. The Wyandotte delegates represented a variety of political views across Kansas Territory. This included radical Republicans, like the ones who had run the Leavenworth convention; more moderate Republicans, like the ones who had run the Topeka convention; and even some Democrats, who had backed the old pro-slavery government.

On those hot summer afternoons, this political cauldron occasionally boiled over. Tempers would flare as shouts of "Liar!" and "Coward!" filled the hall. Delegates even threatened each other with physical violence, egged on by spectators who were separated from the proceedings by a single wooden railing.

During the moments of calm and quiet at the Wyandotte constitutional convention, the attendees would have heard a very different sound — the *click click click* of someone knitting. "Mrs. Nichols sits at the reporter's table every day, some of the time plying her needle, some of the time her pen," wrote the *New York Times* correspondent. The Wyandotte convention, as with most things related to the fate of Kansas, was national news, and Eastern reporters were on hand to cover the proceedings.

One story appearing on the *Times'* front page reported on an after-hours gathering at the Wyandotte City home of Lucy Armstrong, a missionary's daughter married to a Wyandot Indian. She was a long-time leader in the local community, respected by all. Clarina was staying with her and had asked her to host the receptions. As the weary delegates relaxed over coffee and cakes, Nichols did her most important work.

"The hospitable tea table of Mrs. Armstrong offered abundant opportunity for coffee and discussion," Nichols recalled. These independent, strong-minded, highly respected widows made for an awesome twosome.

Nichols would appear each day in her long, plain Sunday dress and take her assigned seat next to the convention chaplain. Reporters started to wonder if she was a Quaker, like Mrs. Mott. Lucy Armstrong was usually in the audience, providing quiet support. Other women attended some days of the convention. Nichols drew strength from her like-minded sisters.

Behind the convention's president, who was seated on a raised platform at one end of the hall, a U.S. flag had been draped. It was a reminder to all that the delegates' main duty was to earn Kansas a star on that flag.

Republicans, who outnumbered the Democrats two-to-one, were in agreement that slavery would be outlawed in Kansas. But they haggled at length over the exact boundaries of the new state. And, once more, they had the nerve to debate whether blacks should be allowed to live and work in Kansas.

Nichols let the men argue. Even before the convention had gotten underway, the response to the petition drive had filled her with confidence. "I felt my wings grow, fearing no disappointment," she wrote Susan B. Anthony.

The old fears of being shamed and ridiculed were long gone. Her age helped protect her, of course, but mostly it was her standing in the community that ensured she would be spared all but the most harmless criticism. The press in attendance generally painted a positive picture of her. The citizens of Wyandotte City, who filled the spectator galleys, also enjoyed her presence. They were used to seeing lawyers, farmers, and merchants arguing over politics. What they weren't accustomed to was a woman in the center of things, calmly knitting through the chaos, taking notes as though she were sitting in the middle of her parlor.

Someone drew up a petition, signed by many of the townfolk, urging the delegates to let Mrs. Nichols address them. "They say I have accomplished a great change in public sentiment," Nichols reported to Anthony. A subcommittee met to consider the matter. One of her supporters scolded the delegates for not letting a woman speak "in her own cause," and reminded them that their

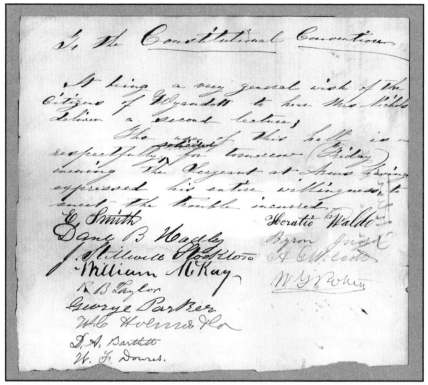

This petition from July 1859, signed by "the citizens of Wyandott[e]," asks for use of the constitutional hall for an after-hours session on women's rights to be led by Clarina Nichols.

mothers had taught them their first lessons in life.

The men of the subcommittee were unmoved, voting down the motion to let Nichols speak during the convention session. Well, someone asked, what about an after-hours session? That seemed like a reasonable compromise to the Republicans. And so, while the Democrats piled into a coach headed for Kansas City and the circus, Nichols addressed the Republican delegates.

The citizens of Wyandotte came to a second evening session where Nichols spoke again. The turnout was large, with many women in attendance, which was a good thing for her, since she had as much work to do convincing women of their rights as she did with men.

Now that her plan had been carried out successfully, she wondered what fruit it would bear. During the early days of the convention, Nichols felt sure that the delegates would be open to granting Kansas women full suffrage. But then, some of her supporters began to sour on that idea. Too radical, they said. It could be used as a reason to keep Kansas out of the Union. A resolution on woman suffrage was voted down. A disappointed Nichols blamed the defeat on "too many old lawyers" — though most of the delegates were in their twenties and thirties.

However, a second proposal did pass, granting women the right to vote in school district elections. Education had always been considered "woman's sphere," and as a former school teacher herself, Nichols was in a strong position to argue that women needed this right so that they could carry out a key responsibility as mothers.

She called the school election amendment "an entering wedge to full suffrage." She was convinced that seeing women vote would end the ridiculous fears people had about suffrage breaking up the traditional family and causing women to neglect their other duties. And then, once everyone was comfortable with school suffrage, the women could approach the Kansas legislature and demand the right to vote in city elections (municipal suffrage), then state elections, then national elections.

In fact, that was exactly how it played out — eventually. It would be another 30 years before Kansas women were given municipal suffrage, and another quarter-century before full suffrage was finally granted in 1912.

Nichols and her supporters gained other historic rights for Kansas women. The Wyandotte Constitution included equal custody rights for women in case of divorce. It granted property rights to married women. And it guaranteed equality of access to education, including the right of women to attend the new state university in Lawrence.

Nichols wrote Anthony with this list of triumphs and setbacks. Anthony wrote back to congratulate her. But the leader of the women's cause out East was realistic about how little had actually been accomplished in Wyandotte, despite the friendly atmosphere.

Anthony wrote, "If it be so in Kansas, the most liberal state in the Union, how is it in the other states?" But that was no longer a concern of Nichols. She had work to do at home.

After the convention she again criss-crossed Kansas Territory, this time seeking support for the new state constitution. She traveled any way she could — with the mail coach, by steamboat, with friends and strangers, by pony, and on foot.

In Atchison, she was invited home by a gentleman who had attended her lecture and wanted to share her message with his wife and three daughters. As it turned out, his wife was not interested in women's rights and scolded her husband for bringing Nichols to their home. The wife could not turn out her unwelcome guest into the streets at so late an hour, so Nichols and her female traveling companion were put up in a sleeping room for the family's hired men.

The two women slept in the middle of three beds, with only a chair on either side separating them from their male sleeping companions. Other hired hands stretched out in bedrolls on the floor. Nichols found the scene highly amusing — at least when she looked back on it.

In Lecompton, men rehearsing for a minstrel show drowned out her lecture, forcing her to cut it short. She was unable to take a collection, which was her usual way of covering her expenses. Finally, four men generously pitched in fifty cents apiece to help cover her costs. And so it went.

In early September she finally met all the members of the Wattles family. Their Moneka Women's Rights Association held back-to-back suffrage and temperance conventions, with Nichols as the featured speaker at both. It would be hard to think of a more radical group of people than those at the Moneka gathering. They believed in total equality between men and women. The only difference they allowed was that women used the pen, the press, and their powers of persuasion to get their way, while men always seemed to require the sword, the rifle, and the cannon.

John Wattles, Susan's husband, was energized by Nichols' talk on suffrage. He called it "one of the most thrilling and convincing" he had ever heard. He had planned to accompany her across Kansas on her speaking tour. But on the final night of the convention, the temperature suddenly plunged. Everyone had dressed for the heat, and people began to shiver. John already had been suffering from a cold, and that night he took to bed with violent tremors. He never recovered. In nine days he was gone.

Now Nichols was without the strong ally who had promised to help her gain support for the Wyandotte Constitution. Once more she would need to carry on alone. It seemed to be her fate in life.

Fortunately, the women's provisions did not seem to bother the white male voters of Kansas Territory. They went to the polls in October 1859 and approved the Wyandotte Constitution by a three-to-one majority. Now all there was to do was wait for new Congress in Washington. Once it was seated in 1861, slavery would be forever abolished in Kansas and free blacks would be allowed to live in the new state.

The passage of the Wyandotte Constitution was cause for patriotic celebrations. Rounds of cannon fire echoed up and down the Missouri River.

But the good news was soon eclipsed by dramatic reports from Harpers Ferry, Virginia, about a bungled plan to liberate slaves that was hatched by a former resident of Kansas Territory.

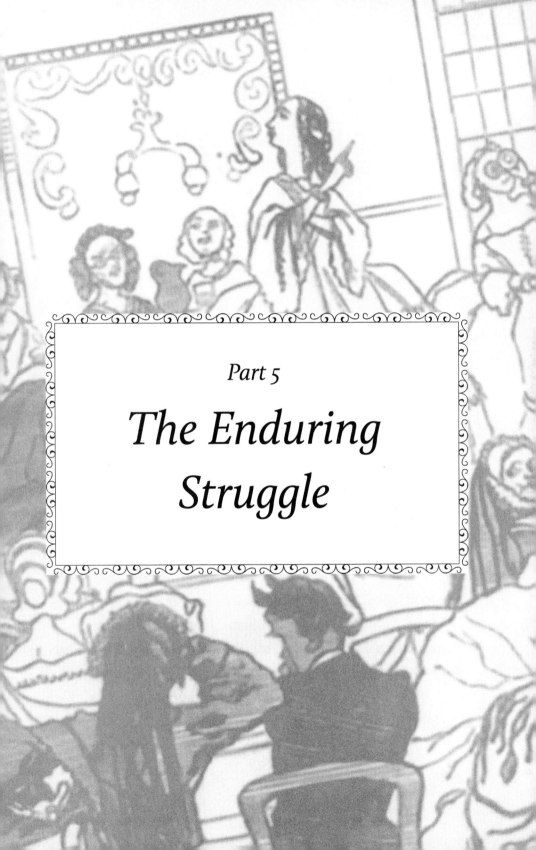

Part 5

The Enduring Struggle

Frontier Justice

On the night of October 16, 1859, John Brown led 21 men on a raid of the federal armory at Harpers Ferry with the intent to distribute all the weapons to slaves in the area and start a rebellion that would wipe slavery from the face of the Earth.

The raid was a fiasco almost from the start. Brown's raiders held the armory for only a few hours before federal troops stormed in. They killed or captured most of the raiders, including Brown. He was tried, convicted, and sentenced to hang on December 2.

Throughout the South, the name John Brown instantly became the symbol of Northern treachery. Among the abolitionists, Brown was already revered for his exploits in the Bleeding Kansas days. Now he was well on his way to sainthood.

Opinion was mixed, though, among more moderate Republicans. Abraham Lincoln, then running for president, chose his words carefully. "Old John Brown has just been executed for treason against a state," he said. "We cannot object, even though he agreed with us in thinking slavery wrong. That cannot excuse violence, bloodshed, and treason."

Nichols was on a lecture tour in Missouri when news of the Harpers Ferry raid arrived. She was scheduled to speak in the pro-slavery border town of Westport that very evening. People were gathering in small groups on the streets, trading news and rumors. Missourians had no trouble believing what Brown had done. They remembered the Pottawatomie Massacre and the raids he had made in their own state to carry off their slaves and "liberate" their cattle. Many believed Brown was part of a broader conspiracy that was just getting started. Across the South and in slave states like Missouri, there was talk about tracking down Brown's allies and stringing them up.

Nichols' lecture that evening was cancelled. The nervous proprietor of the inn where she was staying advised her to leave quickly. She slipped out the back door and headed to safety in Quindaro.

By the beginning of 1860 the boom town had gone bust. Scattered among Quindaro's dwellings were half-finished or abandoned shops, mercantile stores, and homes. Their vacant windows stared out onto dirt streets and a landscape littered with tree stumps, rock piles, and debris. Only the town's hardiest residents were still there, including Nichols and several neighbors she knew she could count on.

The port of Quindaro, Kansas, shown here in a modern painting by Charles Goslin, was located across from the slave plantations in Parkville, Missouri.

This half-empty river town must have been a depressing sight for Lydia Peck as she stepped off the steamboat and started up the hill to the town hotel. But she hadn't come to Quindaro to buy a house or pamper herself on a vacation. She had come for her children.

Like Clarina, Lydia Peck was from New England — and she had also married badly. Unlike Clarina, she was still stuck in the nightmare of her marriage to a man named James Peck. He was abusive and vengeful and lazy and took her wages as quickly as she earned them.

Finally, she had asked him for a divorce — and that was when James Peck showed some initiative. He threw her out of the house, then converted everything she owned into cash and fled with their children, Alma and Liberty. Not only did Lydia have no idea where he had gone, but unlike Nichols she could not call on James's relatives for help. So she did the only thing she could: She went to work in a cotton mill and saved everything she earned until she had enough money to go searching for her children.

Lydia was quite a detective, because she made it over a thousand miles to Quindaro, having learned that James was living there under an assumed name. Soon upon her arrival, Lydia found the one person in town best prepared to help her. As Clarina listened to Lydia's story she realized she knew the man who fit the description of James Peck. It was a man who went by the name of James Dimond, and he was a ne'er-do-well living in a rundown shack down the road with two young children.

Nichols quickly put together a circle of neighbors to help Lydia. At first they thought that several women should try taking the children by force, but Clarina thought better of that idea. James Peck was well-known as a man with a vile temper. The scene could get ugly.

Beyond that, it had already occurred to Clarina that Lydia's plight could serve a larger purpose. James Peck's actions, while extreme, were not illegal. A father who ran off with his children was not breaking the law, at least not in Kansas Territory. However, the Wyandotte Constitution guaranteed equal rights for women in cases of divorce, and Lydia's plight could be a test case of the new law. After all, what Lydia really wanted was a divorce and custody of her children.

After some discussion, the group agreed that Nichols should

travel to the territorial capital and seek a divorce for Lydia, with full custody rights. Packing her "knitting work and reputation," as she put it, Nichols headed for Lecompton.

She stayed for a month, for divorces were no simple matter in Kansas. She kept her eyes on the bill as it worked its way through both houses of the legislature. While the wheels of justice slowly turned, several lawmakers asked the famous champion of women's rights to educate them as to why a wife might need protection from her own husband. Nichols was happy to oblige.

James Peck's attorneys challenged the bill, but they were overruled and the divorce was signed by the territorial governor on February 27, 1860. Lydia Peck had her freedom from James Peck and full custody rights. That should have been the end of the matter. Nichols knew, however, that things were not always as they seemed in Kansas Territory.

Over the winter large numbers of enslaved blacks had crossed over from Missouri into Quindaro. Some of them were captured by unscrupulous Kansas officials, who sold them back to bounty hunters at a tidy profit. If these men felt no guilt about making money off the fugitive slave trade, they certainly would turn a blind eye to a ruling in a child custody case in exchange for a pint of whisky from James Peck.

As soon as the divorce decree was signed, Nichols had a friend with a fast horse race back to Quindaro. The friend alerted the sheriff to be on the lookout for James Peck making a run for the border. Sure enough, as soon as the divorce papers were served, he had grabbed his rifle and his two children and headed for the country. The sheriff arrested him and put Alma and Liberty in the care of a neighbor.

Unfortunately, their father had expected trouble, and had told the children that he had taken them from their mother to keep her from poisoning them. Nichols recalled that Lydia took Alma and Liberty from the neighbor's house "screaming, biting, and scratching their captors." Their mother assured them that she loved them and would never harm them, and at last they believed her. It was after midnight before Mrs. Peck, Alma, and Liberty were spirited out of Quindaro using the escape routes of the underground railroad.

The next day, to keep James Peck from pursuing them, Nichols staged an elaborate charade. She seemed to enjoy cooking up these little dramas, and she was apparently quite a good actor. Her goal was to convince Peck that his children were hidden somewhere in the village. She and her friends spent the next three days walking around Quindaro, looking over their shoulders, huddling together on the street to whisper and exchange notes — in short, to look for all the world like they were up to something. By the time Peck realized he had been tricked, his former family was halfway across the country.

Not willing to admit defeat, he had Nichols and her co-conspirators arrested and charged with "willfully, maliciously, forcibly and fraudulently enticing, leading, carrying away and detaining" Peck's children. What followed was a farce of a trial, which Nichols wrote about to keep her newspaper readers entertained. One report began, "The curtain rises on scene fifth ..."

In the end the case was thrown out, and Nichols had a story she would tell and retell the rest of her life. Best of all, it had a happy ending. She received a letter from Lydia Peck, reporting that she had made it back to New England and was beginning a new chapter in her life. Every night, Nichols reported, Lydia went to bed with her children, "a little sunny head on each arm, because neither was willing to be separated from her."

Interrupted by War

I n the winter of 1861 Nichols and other women's rights advocates were asked to help out in Ohio. Year after year the women of the Buckeye State had been petitioning for a married women's property rights law. This was the year, they believed, that it might actually happen — if they got help. It was not unusual for women's rights workers in one state to put out a call for help to sisters in other states. They all knew each other and kept up with each other's progress.

During the Ohio campaign Nichols met with Frances Gage and Jane Elizabeth Jones, along with Ernestine Rose from New York and Hannah Tracy Cutler from Illinois. They were all veteran reformers, dedicated to temperance, anti-slavery, and women's rights.

The early reformers were connected with one another in many ways. They wrote letters back and forth, stayed at each other's homes while traveling, met one another at conventions, and traveled to each other's states when the call came that a special campaign was underway. They strategized, canvassed, and lectured together, and looked out for each other's children.

Women were brought into the movement by their sisters, mothers, aunts, cousins, in-laws, friends, and schoolmates. As they got older, they passed the torch to the next generation. And so the movement grew.

In Massilon, Ohio, Nichols reported hearing a tragic story. An 8-year-old boy was orphaned by the death of his mother. By law her property was in the hands of her second husband, the boy's stepfather. After laying his beloved to rest, the second husband left town without making any arrangements for the care of his stepson. A good family had taken the boy in and saved him from the poorhouse, but Nichols reminded the public that this situation could have been avoided if the mother had been able to write a will giving her son an inheritance.

Nichols' nine weeks in Ohio paid off when, at long last, the Ohio legislature passed a married women's property rights law.

On her way back to Kansas she made stops in Illinois and Wisconsin to deliver lectures and visit old friends. Everywhere she went, the talk was about civil war. In the weeks since the Republican candidate, Abraham Lincoln, had won the 1860 election, South Carolina had led the secession, or withdrawal, of Southern states from the Union. Other slave states closer to the North, including Missouri, were being urged to join the new Confederacy.

Kansas was finally admitted to the Union on January 29, 1861. Despite clouds on the horizon, the free-state settlers celebrated their hard-fought victory. The new motto of Kansas perfectly described its difficult journey to statehood: *Ad Astra per Aspera* (Latin for "to the stars through difficulties").

Nichols returned to Kansas in late March and made her way to Topeka, where the new state legislature was in session. The town had been deluged by days of rain. It had fallen so heavily, the plaster inside the lawmakers' hall was peeling. Dank clouds of tobacco smoke fouled the air, and many of the lawmakers came down with hacking coughs. Nichols complained of a sore throat that bothered her for weeks.

She met daily with lawmakers, accompanied by a traveling companion identified only as Miss Grant. The two ladies were successful in getting the assembly to pass legislation allowing married women the right to sue and be sued in their own names instead of their husband's. It was yet another way for women to speak up for themselves.

An irritated newspaperman complained about the "everlasting Mrs. Nichols" and her "yoke-mate Miss Grant" and wished they would go back to their knitting. Clarina answered that she would be happy to knit him a pair of socks if he would furnish the yarn.

Once she returned to Quindaro, she found her house in a distressing state of affairs. Rain was pouring into her front room from a leaky roof. She had no funds to repair her house — except for what she had set aside to send Birsha to art school back East. She bought new shingles with the money, and put them on the roof herself.

The downpours of 1861 followed a period of severe drought that had thwarted repeated efforts of the pioneers to feed their families. First the wheat crop failed, so farmers planted corn. When that failed, they dug up the corn and planted buckwheat, and when that too failed, they planted turnips — and even those failed.

The weather extremes were too much for many settlers. They began to abandon their farms in droves. Nichols traveled upriver to Atchison and saw relief supplies from other states once again being handed out to suffering Kansans.

Hollow-cheeked farmers were arriving from the country in empty wagons. She described the scene for readers of the *Chicago Tribune*. "Three out of four are afflicted with the scurvy, some to the extent that their teeth could be taken out with the fingers," she wrote. Nichols and others helped raise awareness of this new crisis, and brought about a massive relief effort.

Would Kansas always need to rely on outside help to survive? It was a fair question. Those years were hard for almost everybody who lived there. Political unrest made investments uncertain. In Quindaro, fortunes were made and lost in a matter of weeks. In Wyandotte City, the price of land swung between $4 and $58 an acre over a six-year period.

Nichols had sacrificed most of her lecture income by moving to Kansas, where she earned only occasional honoraria, and the Moneka Women's Rights Association paid her just enough to cover expenses. At home she took in a gentleman boarder, collected tuition for the schools she and Birsha ran, and sold butter and eggs from her farm. She may also have earned money from her

A *Harper's Weekly* sketch from 1865 shows female clerks leaving work at the U.S. Treasury Department during the Civil War.

newspaper writing.

Like the great majority of pioneers, she was self-sufficient, producing and preserving the food she needed, using the wood on her property for fuel, and bartering with her neighbors for goods and services she did not have. Her expertise at knitting and her skill with the needle helped keep her family's clothing in good repair. She bought a sewing machine at a substantial discount by agreeing to endorse it in the newspaper.

As a well-read, self-educated individual, Nichols found living comfortably in Kansas a challenge. She cut back on reading material and writing paper only when it was absolutely needed to make ends meet. Not having fresh reading material must have been especially painful for her. The arrival of new books and magazines, she recalled later, were like "food that went to the hungry spot." She read her treasured books over and over until the bindings were worn.

Quindaro was soon drained of its military-age men. This included Clarina's older son Howard, who joined the Union Army. From across the river in Parkville, Nichols began hearing enemy soldiers changing guard in the night. Missouri stayed with the Union, but slavery remained legal there until the war's end, and many in western Missouri openly flew the Rebel flag and supported the Confederacy.

She continued to tend her gardens and care for her livestock. "I think I feel the death of favorite animals more than many," she confessed. She was fond of animals and gave names to some of them. Her two cows she named Old Polly and Curly.

After Quindaro's only doctor joined the Union Army, people turned to Clarina for help when they were sick or injured. "Our people are many, and most of them too poor to send out of town," she wrote Susan Wattles. Though she had no formal training in medicine, her mixture of common sense and optimism and her knowledge of substances like arnica and belladonna served her well. She treated her patients with diet and bed rest, various herbal remedies, and hot and cold packs of water.

"I have had several severe cases, one given up by a Wyandotte physician, a pregnant woman in fever — but all have recovered," she reported with satisfaction to Wattles. Her medical services were available to all, regardless of color. Speaking of the woman she had helped through a difficult pregnancy, she said, "She has a fine boy two months old — a black boy — the first free child out of 11 now in slavery."

Meanwhile back East, the Republicans had asked Susan B. Anthony, Elizabeth Cady Stanton, and other women's rights leaders to put their campaign on hold until the war against the South could be won. They agreed to do so. But they did not stop organizing.

In 1863 Anthony, Stanton, and others formed a committee called the Woman's Loyal League. Members began circulating a nationwide petition demanding that President Lincoln free all slaves. The Emancipation Proclamation, issued earlier that year, had freed the slaves in the Confederacy — but not in Missouri or the other slave states that had remained with the Union. An astounding 400,000 signatures, including Nichols', were collected by the Loyal League and delivered to Congress on two enormous spools.

Twice Nichols was warned to flee Quindaro when the war came too close to its borders. She had her carpetbags packed, ready to go at a moment's notice. Old men became patrol guards along the river. They watched night and day for any sign of a coming attack. Residents deserted homes and businesses and moved to safer towns. "We expect trouble if the river freezes," Nichols wrote Susan Wattles. "If I am burned out or driven away I don't know which way I would go."

She sent George, now a teenager, off to school in Baldwin City, Kansas, far from the Missouri border. Birsha went back East to stay with friends. Relie was at the other end of the country, in California. Only Howard's wife Sarah was nearby. For a time she stayed in Quindaro with the couple's two small children, Charles and Irena. Both women had pioneered in Kansas and knew how to take care of themselves under the most difficult circumstances. "She's no mouse," Nichols said approvingly of her daughter-in-law.

But even that relationship was interrupted by the war. Sarah left to become a laundress in the army, so she could earn some money and be near her husband. Once more Clarina was alone.

During the Civil War, women became nurses on the battle-front. They turned their homes into miniature factories to produce uniforms, blankets, bandages, bullets, and other supplies. Some became scouts and spies, and hundreds disguised themselves as men and served as soldiers. Both in the North and the South, women worked the farms and carried on trades and businesses emptied out by the war machine's unending need for more men.

The federal government began recruiting women to fill the posts vacated by men who had gone off to war. Nichols realized this was an opportunity to get out of harm's way, reunite with her daughter, and earn some needed cash.

The two women were among the first female clerks in the Treasury and Army Quartermaster's departments. Nichols, happy to have a paying job and the chance to meet other women, joined the Ladies National Covenant. This group of leading socialites and political wives had organized a boycott of nations supporting the South. The boycott focused on England, which was still doing business with the Confederacy.

At one meeting Nichols attended, the ladies were discussing how to proceed. Someone proposed that a notice go out urging women not to buy imported clothing for the Fourth of July "unless it was absolutely necessary." Nichols objected. She said this would only encourage women to get their holiday shopping done early. Why not start the boycott immediately? Others argued the opposite point, that this was too harsh a demand to make of women.

A reporter from Detroit described what happened next: "Here Kansas came to the rescue again and delivered a stirring little speech, full of pith and patriotism." Nichols reminded the ladies that soldiers were sacrificing far more on the battlefield. She asked if it was really so hard for the women to deny themselves for the sake of the country. After some discussion, the ladies agreed, and the boycott was on.

The Campaign of '67

After the Union's victory in 1865, Nichols — like all females who worked for the federal government during the war — was out of a job. The boys were home, and they took back their old posts. She agreed to become the matron at a Georgetown home for black orphans and widows. The following year her mother died, and she returned to Vermont.

When she finally arrived in Quindaro in early 1867, she saw a depressing sight. Union cavalry had been quartered there throughout the war. Soldiers of the Second Kansas Infantry had camped nearby, tearing down deserted buildings and using the scraps for firewood. Nichols decided to bid Quindaro farewell. She had bought a small farm outside town and prepared to move.

Her plans were interrupted by a dramatic development in Topeka. The service of African-American soldiers in the war had created support for the idea of giving black men the right to vote. The Kansas legislature decided it was a question for the voters to decide. A black suffrage amendment passed both houses and was put on the ballot for a statewide vote that November.

But the question of woman suffrage had not gone away. After some discussion, the Kansas legislature put that amendment on the ballot as well. For the first time in American history, both suffrage questions would be put to a vote by the white male electorate. Nichols was confident her adopted state was about to reward all her efforts on behalf of women. "The hour of universal freedom is coming to us without violence," she wrote in a Vermont newspaper in February.

Women's rights leaders in the East were ecstatic. They made plans to come west to campaign for the cause. In early April the Kansas Impartial Suffrage Association formed. Its goal was to support both amendments. Nichols was at the organizing meeting, along with Lucy Stone and her husband, Henry Blackwell, who had just arrived from New Jersey.

Suddenly a wild-eyed man — "with a hole in his coat and only one shoe," as Nichols recalled — crashed the proceedings. "If I was a Negro, I would not want the woman hitched to my skirts!" he cried. The women hushed him and the meeting went on, but it was a sign of things to come.

Stone and her husband set off on a lecture tour of Kansas. They were delighted by the lovely spring weather and happily surprised by the support they found across the state. It was the same optimistic spirit that had kept Nichols going despite hard times. "This is a glorious country," Henry Blackwell wrote to Elizabeth Cady Stanton. "If we succeed here, it will be the State of the Future." They urged their friends out East to join them.

The Impartial Suffrage campaign was national news. Eastern journalists set out for Kansas once more. The famed Hutchinson Family Singers also made the trek. Their close harmonies had made them one of the most popular singing groups in the nation. For the 1867 campaign they composed "The Kansas Suffrage Song." The lyrics were set to the tune of the folk song "Old Dan Tucker." The chorus went like this:

> *Clear the way, the songs are floating;*
> *Clear the way, the world is noting;*
> *Prepare the way, the right promoting*
> *And ballots, too, for woman's voting!*

Crowds at the Impartial Suffrage rallies were large and enthusiastic. If the election had been held in the spring, both amendments might have passed handily. But then leading Republicans started to have second thoughts. Longtime supporters of woman suffrage like Horace Greeley and Frederick Douglass pulled back. This was the "Negro's hour," they argued — a time to honor thousands of black soldiers who had fought in the Civil War.

The party line changed. Republicans supported black male suffrage but opposed woman suffrage. Even the leaders of the anti-slavery movement came out against woman suffrage. This was especially hard on the women. They had been promised a reward for all their efforts in opposing slavery and supporting the Union during the Civil War. Now they were being snubbed by their old friends. They were furious. The women felt like they had been double-crossed. By fall there was an Anti-Female Suffrage Association with support from both political parties.

Articles began appearing in the local press against the women's amendment. Personal attacks were made on the outsiders who had come to support woman suffrage. A Kansas politician attacked Lucy Stone, accusing her of being in favor of "free love." He declared, "She don't believe in marriage for life, but wishes all to do like her and that seed-wart she carries around with her — called Blackwell." In fact, Lucy and Henry had been married for 12 years, but Stone had kept her maiden name and had the words "promise to obey" struck from her wedding vows.

Nichols was too well known and respected in Kansas to draw that kind of attack. Instead she focused her efforts on the group that she felt could make or break the amendment campaign: ministers of the gospel. She had been debating clergymen from the beginning of her political career, and she knew exactly what Bible passages these men used to make their case.

One story the ministers always emphasized was Eve's role in bringing sin into the world. They were also likely to quote St. Paul's words, telling wives to submit to their husbands. Ministers used their pulpits effectively, as can be seen in the diary entry of a 12-year-old Lawrence girl.

"I think it is against the Bible and the will of God for a woman to take a man's place," she wrote. "I think the men will not respect the women, and that they will neglect their duties."

Nichols was working on a long essay she intended to circulate titled, "The Bible Position of Woman, or Woman's Rights From a Bible Stand-Point." She used humor when it suited her purpose. "There is not one word in the Bible about woman suffrage," she said. "Neither is there one word about apple dumplings. I don't believe they had any in Paul's day, nor man suffrage either, for there is not a word in the Good Book about suffrage for anybody."

She was a believer in an idea that she had first heard about at the First National Woman's Rights Convention in 1850 — "co-sovereignty." It was the idea that men and women shared responsibility for God's creation equally, and were called to share power as partners. It was a radical idea, and Nichols was not shy about sharing it in churches across Kansas.

The summer of 1867 brought more hardships. Grasshoppers devoured Nichols' crop, and she was forced to replant late in the season. She and other family members were sick for a long stretch. When she was not sick, she was helping in Birsha's summer school and packing for her move out of Quindaro.

With all of that going on, she still managed to bring her message on horseback to every house in her county that spring and summer, and spent four weeks in the late summer canvassing several counties for both amendments. She received $50 from the Moneka Women's Rights Association for her services.

But the forecast for both amendments began to turn grim. In other parts of the state women were having a rough time. Racist as well as sexist attacks began to appear in the newspapers. One reporter asked his readers to imagine 400 black women coming to vote, each one "carrying a squalling brat in her arms."

Nichols fired back that the so-called "brat" was the reason all women needed to vote. How else could they protect their "home interests"? What motive did they have to improve themselves and take their rightful place in society?

As the campaign wore on, female suffrage and black male suffrage were pitted against each other. Each side blamed the other for dragging them down. Both causes suffered. Terrible things were said, and the campaign began to wear on everyone's nerves.

German Kansans opposed woman suffrage out of fear that a fresh influx of female voters would pass laws banning alcohol and leave them without beer. Rural Kansans feared that giving black men suffrage would encourage poor blacks to move to Kansas and take jobs away from white Kansans. Newspaper editors claimed that both amendments were too radical for such a young state.

By the time Susan B. Anthony and Elizabeth Cady Stanton arrived in early fall, the campaign for black male suffrage was in jeopardy, and the woman suffrage campaign was in disarray. With little money and dwindling support, Anthony and Stanton made a decision that would taint their reputations and split the movement. They accepted help from George Francis Train, a flashy businessman who was both a supporter of women's rights and a racist opponent of black suffrage.

Anthony's and Stanton's decision caused a furor in Kansas. They tried pointing out that the supporters of black male suffrage took money from people who attacked women. They resented any criticism from men who had once supported the women's cause. Above all, they believed until the very end that they could win Kansas with an all-out, last-ditch, no-holds-barred campaign financed by Train.

Throughout their travels through the state in the fall of 1867, the Eastern women found themselves roughing it to a degree they had not imagined. "The dirt, the food!!" Stanton exclaimed in a letter home. They seemed unaware that these were everyday facts of life to Nichols and other Kansas women. Stanton patted herself on the back for enduring pioneer hardships "with a great deal of cheerfulness."

The black amendment was defeated by a vote of 10,483 for and 19,421 against. The women's amendment lost by an even wider margin: 9,070 for and 19,857 against.

For black male suffrage, this turned out to be a temporary setback. Three years later, passage of the Fifteenth Amendment gave black men the vote, though it would take nearly a century before this right was honored in the Southern states. Despite their many years of working to end slavery, Anthony and Stanton opposed the amendment because it failed to include women. Nichols, though disappointed, supported the black male amendment. She said that black male suffrage was an advance, and for that reason she would support it. Half a loaf, she reasoned, is better than none.

But the bitterness of the 1867 Kansas campaign would not go away. In 1870 the world's first women's rights movement split in two. Many women stayed with the Republican Party in support of black male suffrage. But Stanton and Anthony led the others in a revolt that resulted in the formation of a competing group, the National Woman Suffrage Association. It would be 20 years before the two sides could be convinced to reunite.

There Can Be No Failure

L etters came from California, urging her to go west —
even further west than Kansas. Relie and Helen assured her that the winters were less harsh in Mendoci-
no County, and that she could garden all year round.
And instead of traveling by horse and wagon as once had, Clarina
could use the same transport that had brought President Grant to
Kansas in 1868, when she had approached the general and urged
him to give women the vote.

She had seen the young state of Kansas through its troubled
labor and delivery. Now that it was a strapping ten-year-old, she
felt she could leave it behind forever.

Her oldest son, Howard, had no interest in moving west. He
was settled in Kansas with a wife, children, and a business to take

care of. Birsha had moved back to Vermont after marrying a Civil War general, a widower with three small children. A year later Clarina was still dealing with the hole Birsha's departure had made in Clarina's life. "I seem to have lost power to make sunshine," she said to a friend.

Much as she missed her daughter, the thought of moving back East had no appeal for Clarina. Howard was doing just fine in Kansas. It was George who needed her help. He had been struggling to support his young bride, a Wyandot Indian named Mary Warpole. She had given birth to three children before she was 20 and was often in ill health. George thought the California climate might improve her health — as well as his fortunes.

In 1868 the Wyandots and other Kansas tribes signed the last of the treaties transferring their lands to the federal government. It had been 14 years since the Kansas-Nebraska Act had opened the area for white settlement, on lands that the Indians had been given in previous treaties. Now they agreed to move to new reservations further south, in the territory that would become Oklahoma. Delawares, Kanzas, Kickapoos, Miamis, Osages, Ottawas, Sacs and Foxes, Shawnees, Wyandots, and other smaller tribes were all removed to the new territory.

That made the Green Corn Festival of 1868 a bittersweet occasion, for it would be the last one in Kansas. For as long as anyone could remember, the Wyandots had held the festival every fall to celebrate the corn harvest and to remember the day they had accepted Christianity. Wyandots were respected farmers, merchants, and public officials in Kansas. They had adopted the ways of their white neighbors and had married into white families.

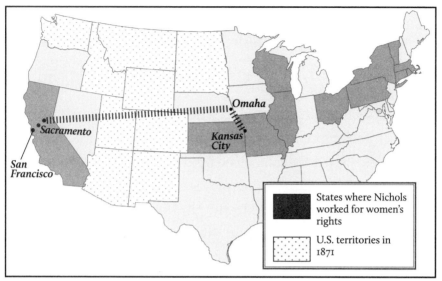

Clarina Nichols worked for women's rights from coast to coast in an era when interstate travel was arduous. On her journey to California in 1871, the tracks from Sacramento to San Francisco were washed out by floods, so train passengers were put on a steamboat — which promptly got stuck.

None of this saved them from the fate of all the other Indians in Eastern Kansas. Those Wyandots unwilling to give up their tribal identities for United States citizenship were forced to leave Kansas for Oklahoma.

In her newspaper report, Nichols wrote that the gathering for the festival was large, respectable, orderly, and without the whole-sale smoking of tobacco that made the Fourth of July celebration an "endurance" for people like her. Wyandot leaders recited the long saga of their people from Canada, where they were part of the Hurons, to Ohio, Michigan, and finally to Kansas.

The festival concluded with dancing. Nichols could not take her eyes off the older women taking part. "They moved in a circle outside the men, erect, calm, dignified and self-possessed, with bowed heads and grave, pensive faces that I will not soon forget."

She wrote an embarrassed letter to Susan B. Anthony cancelling her subscription to Anthony's newspaper, *The Revolution*. Nichols explained that she owed $250 in back taxes and her only source of income at the moment was selling butter and eggs.

"Ah, Susan," she wrote bitterly. "You are a favored individual, to be allowed to fight a big fight. These petty struggles are hateful, belittling."

To save money, she traveled third class on the train to California. This was the compartment mostly used by poor immigrants to America. A friend had assured her that third class would be more roomy than first or second class, and far cheaper. She found she enjoyed the camaraderie with the other people traveling in her car. Several were well-read and could discuss any topic "with sense and feeling," Clarina recalled. "All together we were a sort of family party."

They arrived on New Year's Day, 1872. Relie had settled in the city of Ukiah, northeast of San Francisco. Clarina, George, and Mary opted to settle on land Relie owned in Pomo, 20 miles away in the Potter Valley. Nichols soon had her poultry business up and running again, selling chickens and eggs to buyers who came to her door. Six months later she was expanding the business, building dry sheds and shelters for setting and hatching eggs in the coming winter months.

Alas, the change in climate was not enough to save Mary Warpole. She died a year after they arrived in California at age 24, leaving three small children for her husband to raise. Birney, Clarina's fragile grandson, followed his mother to the grave five years later at age 7.

Besides raising and home-schooling George's girls, Clarina had her chicken business, wrote for the *Pacific Rural Press,* kept up a large correspondence with friends across the country, and tutored second-language learners. Except for the chicken business, none of these activities made her any money.

In a letter to Susan B. Anthony some time later, Clarina confided that she had received an offer of marriage from a "tender love [of] life-long acquaintance." She turned him down, though he might have provided a more comfortable life for her in her later years.

She regretted that she had no time to write a memoir. "What a book I might have given to my dear children, relatives, and personal friends," she said.

Throughout 1876 the United States celebrated its 100th birthday. Many in the women's movement saw little reason to celebrate. In 1776 Abigail Adams had declared, "We will not hold ourselves bound to obey laws in which we have no voice or representation." Brave words indeed — but a century had passed and one half of United States citizens still had no political rights.

A gala celebration was planned in Philadelphia to commemorate the nation's first Fourth of July. The women who had been working for 30 years to secure rights for their sex decided to seize the moment. At their May meeting, the National Woman Suffrage Association drafted a "declaration of rights of the women of the United States, and articles of impeachment against the government." Susan B. Anthony wrote to the head of the centennial commission, asking to be seated at the ceremony and to be allowed to present their declaration.

She was told that only officials were invited to the event, and furthermore, this was not the time and place for a protest, even one that took less than a minute's time. Besides, the program had already been printed. Anthony didn't care. She secured a press pass through her brother Daniel, editor of the *Leavenworth Times* in Kansas. Four other women managed to gain entry as well.

When the day came, they took their places in the meeting hall. As a speaker finished an eloquent reading of the Declaration of Independence, the women rose from their seats on cue and began making their way toward the stage.

Unsure how to respond, the military guards, civil officials, and foreign guests who were flanking the speaker's stand gallantly let the women pass. Anthony approached the flabbergasted speaker and presented him with their declaration. At the bottom were the names of what the document declared to be "the oldest and most prominent advocates of women's enfranchisement." Thirty-one women were listed, including Anthony, Lucretia Mott, Elizabeth Cady Stanton, Paulina Wright Davis, Ernestine Rose — and Mrs. C. I. H. Nichols. Although she was in California, 3,000 miles away, she had managed to add her name to the declaration.

As the officer in charge pounded on his podium and futilely called for order, Anthony and the other women fanned out across

In California, Clarina helped George raise his children after their mother died. From left to right, Helen Clarina Nichols, Birney Nichols, Katherine Howard Nichols.

the room. They handed out copies of their declaration to the invited guests. "On every side eager hands were stretched," said an account of the event. Some men even "stood on chairs and called for copies."

Now in total command of the room, Anthony scaled the musicians' platform and began reciting from the declaration as everyone else read along.

"While the nation is buoyant with patriotism, and all hearts are attuned to praise, it is with sorrow we come to strike the one discordant note, on this one-hundredth anniversary of our country's birth," Anthony said in a strong voice. "We ask of our rulers, at this hour, no special favors, no special privileges, no special legislation. We ask justice, we ask equality, we ask that all the civil and political rights that belong to citizens of the United States, be guaranteed to us and our daughters forever."

The stunt had no immediate political effect, and Anthony's National Woman Suffrage Association remained at odds with the other major women's rights organization. But for all who took part in it, the centennial protest was a moment of juicy satisfaction during a long dry spell in the march toward suffrage.

To the end of her days, Clarina Nichols stayed connected to the cause that had given her life its central purpose. Each year she composed a long, carefully crafted letter that was read out loud at the annual meeting of the National Woman Suffrage Association. For the 1880 convention she looked back to 1850, when the world's first women's rights movement found its voice at that giant hall in Worcester.

"With only the right of petition, free speech, and pen," she observed, women had made great strides. "Who can doubt what would have been the influence of women in the past, or what it will be in the future?"

Back then no one was sure where the movement was going. Since then, obtaining suffrage had become the all-consuming goal of the women. It was almost a sacred quest at this point. Nichols knew that she would never see the day of universal suffrage. She was at peace with that. In her letter to the 1880 convention she made a prophecy, one that would be fulfilled in a way she could not have guessed.

"The leaders in the Suffrage Movement may all die," she wrote, but more leaders, "two to one, will spring from the ranks to bear aloft the glorious banner of a free womanhood."

As she was nearing the end of her life, Nichols put together a final puzzle. Over the years she had suffered from bronchial ailments and a "depression of vitality," she wrote in a California newspaper. "I put this and that together, or rather, this and that came together with a rush of recognition." The common denominator had been second-hand smoke. She recalled that in all-female assemblies she was unaffected, for no well-bred female smoked in public. But men puffed on tobacco everywhere — in public buildings, in their homes, in closed carriages, even inside churches.

In an article titled "The Tobacco Fiend," she wrote, "I am satisfied from observation and experience that tobacco is more destructive to health than alcohol." It was a bold declaration from a lifelong supporter of temperance. She warned "all who value God's breath of life" to stay away from both smoking and second-hand smoke.

The article appeared as Nichols took to bed for the last time. Friends and the California half of her family gathered at her bedside. She had stood by them in good times and bad while maintaining a unique connection to the women's rights movement. Now, with time running out, Clarina Nichols wrote one final letter to her old friend and comrade in arms.

Dear Susan,

I am very sick of acute bronchitis. ... My last words in our good work for humanity through its author is, "God is with us — there can be no failure."

Clarina Irene Howard Nichols died peacefully on January 11, 1885, surrounded by family and friends. She was buried with other family members in Potter Valley, California, surrounded by fields, vineyards, upland meadows, and a ring of gently sloping mountains.

The stories of the early women's rights movement have faded from memory. Today few people know no more than the name of Susan B. Anthony. History textbooks overlook the Worcester conventions and other stories of the world's first women's right movement.

Other pioneers remain largely unknown. Frances Wright. Angelina and Sarah Grimké. Lucretia Mott. Jane Swisshelm. Lucy Stone. Ernestine Rose. Sojourner Truth. Antoinette Brown Blackwell. Paulina Wright Davis. Abby Kelley Foster. Frances Dana Gage. Matilda Joslyn Gage. Clarina Nichols. These women were as important to the future of this country and to liberty as the Founding Fathers of the 18th century or the Civil War generals of the 19th.

They did not fight their revolution on battlefields but in the hearts and minds of citizens of both sexes. When the movement started in the years before the Civil War, few thought that women were men's intellectual equals. Even fewer believed females needed the same rights and opportunities as males. Thanks to the work of this sisterhood and many progressive-minded women who followed, large and small shifts have occurred in every institution in American society, from the law, education, and medicine to religion, the family, and male-female relationships.

The movement to win equal rights for women began long before the 20th century, and those who were there at its founding deserve to be remembered today. Clarina I. H. Nichols was one of them. As she followed the western expansion of the United States, she helped spread the idea that all people are created equal. That no one has the right to bully another. That all citizens have the right to vote and be treated fairly. That everyone has the right to go as far in life as her dreams, talent, and hard work will take her. And that together, girls and boys, men and women can make the world better — if they will.

Items that Clarina Nichols carried with her all her life are on display at the Grace Hudson Museum in Ukiah, California. Grace Carpenter Hudson (pictured), daughter of A.O. and Helen McCowen Carpenter, was a distinguished Western American artist.

Epilogue

The only permanent exhibit devoted to the life and work of Clarina Howard Nichols is at the Grace Hudson Museum in Ukiah, California. Her laptop writing desk is on display, as is the brooch woven from her father's and second husband's locks of hair, and other effects. They include a jewelry box that, according to family legend, was given by Mary Todd Lincoln in appreciation of Nichols' service to the Georgetown home after the Civil War.

Today, Nichols' home town features a roadside marker paying tribute to her remarkable life. Perhaps the finest tribute, however, is the Clarina Howard Nichols Center in Morrisville, Vermont. This is a shelter for victims of domestic abuse and rape. She would have been honored to have her name associated with such a sanctuary, though also saddened to know that domestic abuse and violence against women are still enormous problems in this country and almost everywhere in the world. She would have been surprised at how far we have come — and how far we have yet to go.

"The leaders of the Suffrage Movement may all die..."

Clarina Nichols' declaration to the 1880 women's rights convention proved, in her own case, to be prophetic. On the very day that she died — January 11, 1885 — a Quaker family in New Jersey welcomed Alice Paul into the world. Beginning in 1913, a radical wing of the suffrage movement emerged under the leadership of Alice Paul and Lucy Burns. The women staged parades, protests, and hunger strikes that propelled suffrage to the front page of newspapers across the country and ultimately forced Woodrow Wilson to support suffrage. The Nineteenth Amendment to the United States Constitution was passed in 1920, giving American women at long last the right to vote.

A Quick History Of
The World's First Women's Rights Movement

The roots of the world's first women's rights movement can be traced to the Revolutionary War (1775–81). The Founding Fathers claimed that certain "truths" were "self-evident" and that "all men" were political equals. "All men" originally included only a small class of property-owning white men, but other men — and women — soon began trying to expand the definition to include all men, all races, and both sexes. Abigail Adams (1744–1818) had instructed her husband to "remember the ladies" as he and other delegates were writing the Declaration of Independence (1776). They had not.

In England Mary Wollstonecraft (1759–97) published *A Vindication on the Rights of Woman* (1792) in response to Thomas Paine's best-seller, *The Rights of Man* (1791), at the height of the French Revolution. Wollstonecraft's book, which assessed women's current status and the changes she envisioned, influenced all of the pioneers in the movement

Abigail Adams, Mary Wollstonecraft, Frances Wright

that followed. Lucretia Mott (1793–1880), a Quaker minister born the year after *Rights of Woman* was published, read the slim volume until its pages were as worn as those in her Bible. Mott criticized members of the clergy who taught female submission as God's will. Frances Wright (1795–1852), an emigré from Scotland who had no time for organized religion, spoke out publicly on controversial subjects such as race, sex, religion, and birth control. She shocked her U.S. audiences but won admiration from the early women's rights leaders. Ten years later, the Grimké sisters, Sarah (1792–1873) and Angelina (1805–79), renounced their Southern slaveowning roots and took to the Northern abolitionist lecture circuit. Sarah Grimké compared the legal and political status of married women to that of slaves. In 1845 Margaret Fuller (1810-50) published *Woman in the Nineteenth Century,* an instant classic that laid out many of the intellectual arguments for woman's emancipation. By this time individuals in several states had begun working to change laws that automatically divested women of their property upon marriage.

Margaret Fuller, Sarah and Angelina Grimké, Frederick Douglass

Ernestine Rose (1810–92) traversed New York state for a dozen years, collecting petitions for a married women's property rights bill which was finally passed in 1848.

A year earlier, Clarina Nichols (1810–85) helped secure a modest married women's property rights law in Vermont. Nichols' first forays into the public arena were for temperance. In 1826 the first American temperance society was founded. It was dedicated to reform through cutting alcohol consumption. The movement drew massive support from both conservative clergy and radical reformers. Though agreed on the harmful effects of alcohol, the temperance allies did not agree on other social reforms such as abolition and women's rights (the more conservative ministers opposed both). Ultimately, the movement split over the issue of women's equal participation.

In the early 1830s large numbers of people also began joining forces to confront the evil of slavery. William Lloyd Garrison (1805–79), founder of the American Anti-Slavery Society in Boston in 1833, began

Jane Swisshelm, Lucy Stone, Horace Greeley

allowing women full participation in his organization; Abby Kelley Foster (1810–87) was one such prominent member. Garrison's move met with disapproval from members who broke away to form their own anti-slavery society in 1840.

Another great leveling force was journalism. In the mid-19th century newspapers were abundant, cheap, and Americans' main source of national and world news and opinion. Nichols began editing the *Windham County Democrat* around 1843. In another decade, the number of women editing reform newspapers included Amelia Bloomer (1818–94) of *The Lily*, Jane Swisshelm (1815–84) of *The Visiter*, and Paulina Wright Davis (1813–76) of *The Una*. Alliances were formed between the women's movement and progressive newspapermen like Garrison of *The Liberator* and Horace Greeley (1811–72) of the *New-York Tribune*. Combined with their work in the temperance and anti-slavery movements, public speaking, petition drives, and the publication of sympathetic books and tracts, women found numerous ways to educate themselves and others regarding the issues that animated them.

Sojourner Truth, Elizabeth Cady Stanton (and Harriot), Susan B. Anthony

By the late 1840s there was widespread curiosity and interest in the subject of women's rights throughout New England, New York, Ohio, and other Northern states. In 1848 Mott, Elizabeth Cady Stanton (1815–1902), and three other women convened a two-day meeting in Seneca Falls, New York, on women's rights. Though the meeting was called hastily — the organizers had two weeks to publicize it — about 300 were present when Stanton read her Declaration of Sentiments, a watershed manifesto that listed women's grievances and demands. Frederick Douglass (1817–95), the ex-slave turned editor and abolitionist, helped pass the most controversial measure at the convention: woman suffrage. By contrast, a resolution declaring "that woman is man's equal — was intended to be so by the Creator" passed easily.

In 1850 Davis and others called for the First National Woman's Rights Convention in Worcester, Massachusetts. This meeting proved that the new movement was not a regional oddity or a passing concern. Letters of encouragement were received from as far away as England and France. The only pall cast over the convention was the absence of Full-

Antoinette Brown Blackwell, Frances E.W. Harper, Abby Kelley Foster

er, who was expected to play a leading role at the convention but had drowned at sea on her way back to New York from Europe. Sojourner Truth (c. 1797–1883), an abolitionist and former slave, spoke at the convention, as did Douglass. Their early support for women's rights helped link the women's and anti-slavery causes. That same year, the Fugitive Slave Law passed Congress, which made it a crime not only to help runaways but also to refuse to aid their capturers. Women were quick to see a parallel: sheltering or helping a woman fleeing from a drunken or abusive husband was also a crime punishable by fine or imprisonment. During the 1850s and until the outbreak of the Civil War (1861–65), large women's rights conventions were held across the North. Men as well as women were involved. Women's rights study groups formed in small towns and prairie outposts. Susan B. Anthony (1820–1906) entered and quickly became a leader in the emerging women's rights movement. She had been actively involved in both the temperance and anti-slavery causes. Women addressed constitutional conventions in several states. Legislatures began passing married women's property rights laws. In

Lucy Burns, Frances Willard, Alice Paul

1859, due largely to Nichols' influence, the assembly that would produce the Kansas state constitution voted to include property, custody,
and educational rights for women. Kansas also permitted women to
vote in school district elections. The following year, Anthony and Stanton were successful in pressuring New York to pass a comprehensive
Married Women's Property Bill.

In the face of enormous social disapproval and resistance, the ladies
of the world's first women's rights movement relied on ties of kinship
and friendship to support and sustain them. Besides the Grimké sisters,
a remarkable trio of sisters-in-law were Elizabeth Blackwell (1821–1910),
the first female doctor in the U.S.; Antoinette Brown Blackwell (1825–
1921), the first woman ordained by a mainline Protestant Church; and
Lucy Stone (1818–93), a powerful speaker in several reform movements.
Lucretia Mott's sister, Martha Coffin Wright (1806–75), was active in
the movement. Anthony had a sisterly relationship with Stanton that
was extraordinarily strong and productive. And many daughters and
nieces, including Stanton's, Anthony's, and Stone's, carried on the work

when their mothers or aunts died.

During the Civil War, women willingly set aside their campaign for rights in order to help the Union. Stanton and Anthony collected 400,000 signatures for the Woman's Loyal League, which called for the immediate emancipation of slaves. Many, like Nichols, worked in war-related jobs and helped settle and educate former slaves. At war's end the women took up their cause once more. However, their former male allies had abandoned them, as Garrison, Douglass, Greeley and others focused on obtaining suffrage for black men. A universal suffrage campaign in Kansas in 1867 failed to bring the vote to either blacks or women. The Fifteenth Amendment to the Constitution, ratified in 1870, gave suffrage to black men but not women.

Divided and disillusioned over the amendment, the women's rights leaders — who had seen two reform movements divide over gender — saw their own movement divide over race. Women who supported the Fifteenth Amendment and the Republican Party formed the American Woman Suffrage Association, while those opposed joined Anthony and Stanton in their new National Woman Suffrage Association. These two organizations remained separate for the next 20 years. This split, along with the discouraging defeat in Kansas, effectively brought the world's first women's rights movement to an end.

In the final years of the 19th century, a new emphasis on winning suffrage restarted the movement. Frances Willard (1839–98) organized the Woman's Christian Temperance Union in 1874, which called for total prohibition of alcohol and supported woman suffrage. Thousands of less radical women joined the suffrage cause because they saw it as the best way to achieve Prohibition. Western states began granting full suffrage to women, beginning with Wyoming in 1869. The leaders in many of these states were progressive-minded men, but they were also practical-minded men, and the suffrage laws were usually meant to entice

This dramatic illustration by Henry Mayer filled two pages of a popular magazine in 1915. Nearly all state legislatures in the West, as well as Kansas in the Midwest, had by 1915 passed bills legalizing woman suffrage.

women to move to their sparsely populated states.

In 1890 the National and American groups reunited. Frances E.W. Harper (1825–1911) helped found the National Association of Colored Women in 1894. Alice Paul (1885–1977) and Lucy Burns (1879-1966) organized the Congressional Union in 1913. Later known as the National Women's Party, its members took part in parades, pickets, hunger strikes and other attention-getting tactics to publicize "Votes for Women." Their campaign resulted in the passage of the Nineteenth Amendment to the Constitution in 1920, ending the longest-running civil rights campaign in U.S. history.

Victory, however, came at a price. The new movement ignored the goal that was so important to the world's first women's rights movement: that of complete co-sovereignty between men and women. This larger social agenda would not be seriously taken up again until the 1960s.

For Further Reading

Bausum, Ann. *With Courage and Cloth: Winning the Fight for a Woman's Right to Vote.* Washington: National Geographic, 2004.

Chin-Lee, Cynthia. *Amelia to Zora: Twenty-Six Women Who Changed the World.* Watertown: Charlesbridge, 2005.

Cooper, Ilene. *A Woman in the House (and Senate): How Women Came to the United States Congress, Broke Down Barriers, and Changed the Country.* New York: Abrams, 2014.

Johnston, Norma. *Remember the Ladies: The First Women's Rights Convention.* New York: Scholastic, 1995.

Macy, Sue. *Wheels of Change: How Women Rode the Bicycle to Freedom (With a Few Flat Tires Along the Way).* Washington: National Geographic, 2011.

McKissack, Pat. *Sojourner Truth: Ain't I a Woman?* New York: Scholastic, 1992.

Pollack, Pamela D., Meg Belviso, Mike Lacey. *Who Was Susan B. Anthony?* New York: Grosset & Dunlap, 2014.

Stone, Tanya Lee. *Elizabeth Leads the Way: Elizabeth Cady Stanton and the Right to Vote.* New York: Henry Holt, 2008.

Yousafzai, Malala. *I Am Malala: How One Girl Stood Up for Education and Changed the World.* New York: Little, Brown & Company, 2014.

Clarina Nichols in 1843, the year she married George Nichols. And that's me, wearing the same brooch! Her descendant, Janice Parker, brought this beloved family heirloom to Lawrence, Kansas, for me to wear when performing the words of Clarina Nichols at the Bleeding Kansas Chautauqua in 2004.

Acknowledgments

This book and its parent work, *Revolutionary Heart*, were a long time in the making.

I am deeply grateful to the late Joseph Gambone for collecting and annotating Nichols' papers from across the country.

For opening doors, I thank Steve Collins, John Nichols, and Adrianne Christensen.

For her ongoing generosity, thanks to Karen Holmes of the Grace Hudson Museum.

Thanks also to two of Nichols' direct descendants, Juanita Johnson and Patricia Rabinowitz, for family papers and memories, and to Juanita's daughter, Janice Parker, for Clarina's teenage portrait and for making possible the moment described on the facing page.

Special thanks to Marilyn Blackwell and Kristin Oertel for discovering more about Nichols' alter ego, Deborah Van Winkle.

I am obliged to all the museums and historical societies mentioned in the Notes.

Clarina Nichols has been in my life for so long that she feels like part of the family. Thanks to my actual family members for support, love, and humor — Edward, Anne, Cris, Michael, Sofia, Alex, Nico, Malcolm, and Alexandra.

Most of all, thank you, Aaron. I would never have been able to bring this book to completion without your 20/20 vision.

Notes

These notes are condensed from the more extensive notes in the back of my biography of Clarina Nichols, *Revolutionary Heart* (Kansas City: Quindaro, 2006). Abbreviations used in the following notes are:

CIHN   Clarina Irene Howard Nichols

HWS   Stanton, Elizabeth Cady, Susan B. Anthony, Matilda Joslyn Gage, and Ida Husted Harper, eds., *History of Woman Suffrage* (Rochester, New York: Susan B. Anthony and Charles Mann Press, 1881-1922, 6 vols.)

KHQ   *Kansas Historical Quarterly* (Topeka: Kansas State Historical Society); most references are to Gambone, Joseph G., ed., "The Forgotten Feminist of Kansas: The Papers of Clarina I. H. Nichols, 1854-1885," v. 39 and 40 (1972-1973)

KSHS   Clarina I. H. Nichols papers and poetry journal at the Kansas State Historical Society, Topeka; originals are in the collection of the Schlesinger Library, Harvard University

MWRA   Moneka Women's Rights Association papers at the Kansas State Historical Society, Topeka

SBA   Susan B. Anthony

Introduction

Readers may wonder how to pronounce Clarina Nichols' first name. In my interview with Juanita Johnson, she said that her mother, who was Nichols' great-granddaughter, told her to say "Cla-rih-nah" with the "i" sound as in "dinner."

1 "Grant! Grant! Grant!": KHQ, v. 39, p. 550-551.

Vermont Girl

10 Mrs. Howard wanted: KHQ, v. 40, p. 457.

10 "That is Clarina all over — so ingenious!": Letter, Birsha Carpenter to CIHN, October 17, 1848, KSHS.

10 "think so much better to the click": CIHN, *The Lily*, March 1850.

11 Save everything, waste nothing: KHQ, v. 40, pp. 257–258 and v. 40, p. 134.

11 "To keep step to its music": KHQ, v. 40, p. 272.

13 Family members took turns: KHQ, v. 40, p. 127.

13 ghost stories: Ibid.

14 "Oh, my children": KHQ, v. 40, p. 258.

Learning Hard Lessons

15 "I took to learning": KHQ, v. 40, p. 458.

17 Chapin invited her: KHQ, v. 39, p. 247.

17 "I would shrink from myself": Ibid.

18 "Comparative of a Scientific": see Phelps, James H., *Collections Relating to the History and Inhabitants of the Town of Townshend, Vermont* (Brattleboro: G.E. Selleck, 1877), pp. 183–184.

20 girls' brains: Chapin and Aurelius Howard attended a lyceum in West Townshend that debated whether girls had the same capacity for intelligence as boys. The "nays" carried the day. Lyceum records at Vermont Historical Society, Montpelier.

20 feeling nervous: KHQ, v. 40, p. 453.

21 "I had a longing": *Proceedings of the Second National Woman's Rights Convention*, 1851, Worcester, Mass., p. 31.

A Promising Marriage

27 "coffee, tea, and pure, cold water": *Brockport Free Press*, July 6, 1831.

27 "the most pleasing and heart-cheering": Ibid.

New York Trials

28 "by mutual consent": *Brockport Free Press*, March 16, 1831.

30 "Her recreant husband": CIHN, writing as "Annie" in the Atchison (Kansas) *Freedom's Champion*, February 25, 1860.

30 "intelligent mistress": *Freedom's Champion*, February 25, 1860.

30 "this scene of past sorrows": CIHN to "Dear Parents," July 14, 1833, in KSHS.

30 New York City: In Longworth's 1834–35 *New York Register and City Directory*, Justin Carpenter is listed as living at 115 Fulton Street.

31 "I saw a middle-aged, stalwart Methodist": KHQ, v. 40, p. 424.

32 "a treasure sent": CIHN's poetry journal, at KSHS.

33 "Burned out and lost all": Typewritten note added to the Union College (Schenectady, New York) Record for Justin Carpenter, Class of 1830.

34 "defeated purposes": CIHN to SBA, March 24, 1852, KSHS.

34 "malevolent desire to wound": *Freedom's Champion*, February 25, 1860. CIHN wrote as "Annie"; see note above.

34 Birsha: A handwritten note added to one of Clarina Carpenter's poems reads, "Cheer up my daughter." CIHN poetry journal in KSHS.

34 "Aurelius, my son": Ibid.

35 "I cannot love another ... Why do I weep? ... Days of Sorrow": Ibid.

Finding George

36 "a wounded dove": Atchison *Freedom's Champion*, February 25, 1860.

38 "plain person": George Nichols to Clarina Carpenter, February 18, 1843, KSHS.

38 "A jewelry box": Ibid.

38 formally end her marriage to Justin: KHQ, v. 40, pp. 557-8.

38 "cruelty, unkindness, and intolerable severity": Supreme Court of Judicature, State of Vermont, February 16, 1843.

39 Justin's father … stayed in touch: CIHN to SBA, March 24, 1852.

Inventing Deborah

41 "water-cure": For an account of the author Harriet Beecher Stowe's long and successful convalescence at the Brattleboro water-cure in 1846, see Hedrick, Joan D., *Harriet Beecher Stowe: A Life* (New York: Oxford University Press, 1994).

42 Longfellow: CIHN to H. W. Longfellow, November 25, 1845, letter in the collection of Houghton Library, Harvard University.

42 chronic lung condition: George's ailment, which ultimately ended his life, is mentioned in "Death Notices from Kansas Newspapers," KHQ, v. 18, p. 411.

42 Democratic Party: CIHN's correspondence with a relative, Harley Smith, shows her thinking on slavery at this time (letter dated August 15, 1847, in KSHS).

45 "They tell about wimin": *Windham County Democrat*, December 10, 1847.

Seneca Falls

Accounts of the 1840 World Anti-Slavery Convention and 1848 Seneca Falls Convention are in HWS, v. 1, pp. 50-62 and 67-74. Also see "Further Reading."

Coming Out

54 "I know some folks argue …": *Windham County Democrat*, June 2, 1849.

55 "promiscuous" setting: KHQ, v. 40, p. 444.

55 "I am a walking storehouse": CIHN to SBA, March 24, 1852, KSHS.

56 came back to property: CIHN in *The Lily*, September 1850.

58 "the first breath": HWS, vol. 1, p. 172.

59 "My husband wanted …": CIHN to SBA, March 24, 1852, KSHS.

Worcester

The First National Woman's Rights Convention in Worcester is described in McClymer, John, *This High and Holy Moment* (Fort Worth: Harcourt Brace & Company, 1999) and in HWS, v. 1, pp. 215-226. The Worcester Women's History Project (WWHP) has made many documents from the two Worcester conventions available online.

61 "The room was crowded to excess": *New-York Tribune*, October 25, 1850.

62 "In many countries we see women": *Proceedings of the National Women's Rights Convention*, Worcester, Mass., 1850.

63 "the million and a half of slave women": Ibid.

Clarina Speaks

The text of "On the Responsibilities of Woman" can be found at archive.org. It was originally published as *Series of Woman's Rights Tracts No. 6* (Rochester: Steam Press of Curtis, Butts & Co., 1854).

64 "You must speak now": KHQ, v. 40, p. 556.

70 "many eyes all unused to tears": HWS, v. 1, p. 218.

72 "Only those who have suffered": *Burlington Courier*, November 25, 1852.

Gaining Courage

73 Susan B. Anthony: "I love Mrs. Stanton & all the faithful workers, but it seems to me that we two more than any I know, live in this woman movement because we see in it the divine development of humanity as a whole" (CIHN to SBA, August 21, 1881, quoted in KHQ, v. 40, p. 513).

75 "It is most invigorating": *The Life and Work of Susan B. Anthony*, v. 1, by Ida Husted Harper (Indianapolis: The Hollenbeck Press, 1898), p. 66.

76 "We can't understand": *Windham County Democrat*, undated clipping.

78 "molested by rowdy": *Windham County Democrat*, undated clipping.

79 "Have you the nerve?": *Pacific Rural Press*, January 29, 1881.

79 "If the lady wants to make herself": HWS, v. 1, p. 173.

80 "law adopted by bachelors": Ibid.

80 "muffled thunder of stamping feet": Ibid., p. 174.

80 "We did not know" and "unsex herself": Ibid.

The World Is on the Move

82 "The Crystal Palace is a symbol": *New York Times*, July 14, 1853.

84 James McCune Smith: HWS, v. 1, p. 512.

85 "I say that woman is the greatest sufferer": *New York Times*, September 3, 1853.

85 "the most spirited and able": quoted in HWS, v. 1, p. 511.

86 "We saw, in broad daylight": *New York Herald*, September 7, 1853, quoted in HWS, v. 1, p. 556.

87 "The mayor promised": Ibid., p. 573.

88 "In the Green Mountain State": Ibid., p. 563.

88 "My husband wishes me to vote": Ibid., p. 561.

88 "Where did your Christ come from?": Karlyn Kohrs Campbell, *Man Cannot Speak for Her: A Critical Study of Early Feminist Rhetoric* (New York: Praeger, 1989), v. 1, p. 21.

88 "You may hiss as much as you like": HWS, v. 1, p. 568.

89 "several gentlemen" apologized: *The Liberator*, September 30, 1853.

Winning Wisconsin

Nichols' reports on her Wisconsin trip appeared in the *Windham County Democrat*, October 5 and 12, 1853.

92 "You will be doing just the work": HWS, v. 1, p. 178.

93 "stooping to the most disgusting depths": HWS, v. 1, p. 179.

94 "joyfully welcome": *Milwaukee Daily Free Democrat*, September 27, 1853.

95 voted to support: *Chicago Daily Tribune,* September 30, 1853.

95 "We hereby give notice": *Milwaukee Daily Free Democrat*, September 30, 1853.

95 "Broad prairies, gallant lakes": *Windham County Democrat*, October 12, 1853.

96 church in Waukesha: HWS, v. 1, pp. 180–182.

A Country Divided

"Letters of the Rev. Samuel Young Lum, Pioneer Missionary, 1854-58" (KHQ, v. 25, pp. 39-67) gives a vivid description of early life in Lawrence.

100 close down the *Democrat:* see the notice in *The Liberator*, February 3, 1854.

100 "I told you, ladies and gentlemen": HWS, v. 1, p. 175.

100 "masculine brawler": HWS, v. 1, p. 175.

101 "Don't take away my children!": *Brattleboro Eagle*, February 24, 1854.

101 "My friends!": HWS, v. 1, p. 176.

104 "a great moral wrong": *The Liberator*, March 10, 1854.

104 "conservative old Vermont": KHQ, v. 40, p. 512.

Meat, Mush, Molasses

107 "Picture the writer" and "snatches of song": Boston *Evening Telegraph*, October 31, 1854, quoted in KHQ, v. 39, p. 29.

107 "a pious doctor": HWS, v. 1, p. 185.

108 "Can you tell me where all these people": Ibid. p. 195.

108 Kansas City: KHQ, v. 39, p. 32.

110 loud cheering: HWS, v. 1, pp. 185–186.

111 "as I have seldom": KHQ, v. 39. p. 37.

111 "a group of men standing around": KHQ, v. 39, p. 40.

112 "The climate is the finest": Ibid., p. 41.

113 "The women are 'strong-minded'": KHQ, v. 39, p. 33.

113 "But that was all *head* knowledge": KHQ, v. 39, p. 38.

113 "Do not expect to eat oysters": A.O. Carpenter, *Vermont Phoenix*, May 5, 1855.

Prairie Home

115 "Mrs. Nichols is yet hopeful": *Vermont Phoenix*, February 3, 1855.

115 "God only knows": Birsha Carpenter to CIHN, undated, KSHS.

116 pioneer woman's trunk: KHQ, v. 25, p. 107.

117 "as if such things as surveyed roads": CIHN in KHQ, v. 39, p. 220.

118 "solitude of the prairies" : CIHN in KHQ, v. 39, p. 221.

118 "I liked this region of country": Ibid.

118 "fewer and farther apart than were angels' visits": KHQ, v. 39, p. 38.

120 "Our dinner was spread": KHQ, v.39, p. 228, f.n. 17.

121 "I know what a good husband is": CIHN to SBA, March 24, 1852, KSHS.

121 "with the tenderness of a woman": CIHN handwritten note on letter dated November 28, 1870, to A. O. Carpenter, KSHS.

Tinderbox

124 Missourians: KHQ, v. 39, p. 52.

126 "Sharps rifles are in all our cabins": KHQ, v. 39, p. 232.

127 "fearful silence": KHQ, v. 40, p. 128.

127 convinced the mail carrier: KHQ, v. 39, p. 233.

127 "I hung it there, but my wife": Ibid., p. 234.

Bleeding Kansas

130 "The black male and the white females": KHQ, v. 39, p. 240.

130 "Nobody out here": *Herald of Freedom*, August 11, 1855.

130 "tyrannies and oppressions" and "claim no relationship to the African": *Herald of Freedom*, August 25, 1855. A.O. Carpenter chimed in with an article the following week poking fun at the Back Woodsman. Exchange cited in Blackwell, Marilyn S., *Frontier Feminist: Clarina Howard Nichols and the Politics of Motherhood* (with Kristen T. Oertel,

Lawrence: University of Kansas Press, 2010), pp. 156–157.

132 Charles Robinson: "Message to the Senate by Franklin Pierce," in the *Records of the U.S. Senate* for January 24, 1856, pp. 74–79.

132 Sumner's speech on "the Harlot Slavery" was entered into the *Records of the U.S. Senate*, May 19-20, 1856.

132 dumped the *Herald's* presses: HWS, v. 2, p. 189.

133 "The late news from Kansas": quoted in KHQ, v. 39, p. 253.

133 "crazy — crazy": quoted in "John Brown's Body," by Adam Gopnik, *The New Yorker*, April 25, 2005, p. 90.

135 "My son lives to fight another day": KHQ, v. 39, p. 254.

136 "so poorly clad": KHQ, v. 39, p. 258, f.n. 76.

136 "Poor bleeding Kansas — how the soul sickens": KHQ, v. 39, p. 2, f.n. 69.

137 "Are you mothers?": KHQ, v. 39, p. 259.

137 "Don't ever tell me": Broadside in KSHS.

137 "whose whole souls were in the movement": KHQ, v. 40, p. 452.

138 "And Wisconsin": HWS, v. 1, p. 632.

Quindaro

139 "charity tea": *Quindaro Chindowan*, May 30, 1857.

140 "good housewifery": KHQ, v. 40, p. 538.

141 "The violent thunderstorms are enough to wreck the nerves": *Ho for California!*, edited by Sandra L. Myres (San Marino: Henry Huntington Library and Art Gallery, 1980), pp. 95–96.

142 Clarina was ready: See her letter to Sara T. D. Robinson, September 25, 1882, quoted in KHQ, v. 40, p. 533.

142 "a hundred buildings — many of them of stone": KHQ, v. 40, p. 539.

144 "Of the many slaves who took the train of freedom": KHQ, v. 40, p. 541.

Caroline

For CIHN's account of the incident with Caroline, see KHQ, v. 40, p. 541–542.

148 "blessed events": CIHN to Susan Wattles, June 3, 1860, in MWRA. On January 24, 1858, Samuel F. Tappan, a free-state emigrant based in Lawrence, wrote the noted journalist T. W. Higginson, "I am happy to inform you that a certain Rail Road has been and is in full blast. Several persons have taken full advantage of it to visit their friends." Letter at KSHS.

148 "To the hunt!": KHQ, v. 39, p. 430.

149 "starving for our principles": CIHN to Susan Wattles, May 2, 1859, MWRA.

149 "Go to the grand old woods": *Quindaro Chindowan*, June 27, 1857.

150 "dawn of freedom on her glorious prairies": KHQ, v. 39, p. 410.

151 "Many a brave deed was done there": KHQ, v. 40, p. 529.

Wyandotte

153 insert women's rights into a state constitution: CIHN was not alone in thinking Kansas could make history. "It is not at all impossible that Kansas may set a brilliant example to the rest of the world" (*New York Times*, July 22, 1859, quoted in KHQ, v. 39, p. 24).

153 "do no good": CIHN to Susan Wattles, May 2, 1859, in MWRA.

153 "with great pleasure": Susan Wattles to CIHN, May 4, 1858, in MWRA.

154 "To feel perfectly": CIHN to Susan Wattles, March 29, 1859, in MWRA.

154 "There is no man to go with me": KHQ, v. 39, p. 414.

154 "I am in perfect trim": Ibid., p. 415.

157 "Mrs. Nichols sits at the reporter's desk": *New York Times*, June 22, 1859.

157 "The hospitable tea-table of Mrs. Armstrong": KHQ, v. 40, p. 438.

158 "I felt my wings grow": KHQ, v. 39, p. 415.

158 "in her own cause": John Ritchie, in *Proceedings of the Kansas Constitutional Convention*, Wyandotte, 1859, p. 73.

158 "They say I have accomplished": KHQ, v. 39, p. 420.

160 The turnout was large: KHQ, v. 39, p. 417, f.n. 61.

160 "too many old lawyers": HWS, v. 1, p. 194.

161 "If it be so in Kansas": KHQ, v. 40, p. 114, f.n. 52.

Frontier Justice

161 In Atchison: KHQ, v. 40, pp. 559–560.

162 "one of the most thrilling": Lawrence *Republican*, September 29, 1859.

166 "Old John Brown": *The Collected Works of Abraham Lincoln*, Roy P. Basler, editor (New Brunswick: Rutgers University Press, 1953), v. 3, p. 502.

167 Westport: HWS, v. 1, p. 197–198.

169 James Dimond: *Pacific Rural Press*, September 7, 1878, v. 16, p. 150.

169 "knitting work": *Pacific Rural Press*, December 7, 1878, v. 16, p. 358.

170 unscrupulous Kansas officials: KHQ, v. 39, p. 427.

171 "screaming, biting, and scratching": Ibid., p. 429.

171 "willfully, maliciously, forcibly and fraudulently": "Quindaro" to Lawrence *Republican*, March 29, 1860.

171 "The curtain rises": Ibid.

171 case was thrown out: Ibid., June 28, 1860.

171 "a little sunny head on each arm": KHQ, v. 39, p. 429.

Interrupted by War

175 "The everlasting Mrs. Nichols": KHQ, v. 39, p. 430. CIHN's retort in Ibid., p. 431.

176 abandon their farms in droves: See KHQ, v. 39, p. 441.

176 "Three out of four are afflicted with the scurvy": KHQ, v. 39, p. 437.

177 make ends meet: CIHN to Susan Wattles, March 27, 1859, in MWRA.

177 "food that went to the hungry spot": KHQ, v. 39, p. 542.

178 "I think I feel the death of favorite animals": CIHN to Susan Wattles, October 21, 1861, in MWRA.

178 "Our people are many": Ibid.

178 "I have had several severe cases": Ibid.

178 "She has a fine boy two months old": Ibid.

179 "We expect trouble if the river freezes": Ibid.

179 "She's no mouse": Ibid.

180 Ladies National Covenant: *New York Times*, May 5, 1864.

181 "absolutely necessary": This meeting is recorded in Adams, Lois Bryan, *A Letter from Washington* (monograph, Wayne State University Press, 1999), p. 135.

181 "Here Kansas came to the rescue again": Ibid., p. 136.

The Campaign of '67

For more on the 1867 Impartial Suffrage Campaign see HWS (v. 2, pp. 229–268), KHQ ("With the Help of God and Lucy Stone," v. 35, pp. 13–26), and the "Campaign of 1867" file in the Woman Suffrage History Collection, KSHS.

183 "The hour of universal freedom is coming": KHQ, v. 39, p. 517.

183 "with a hole in his coat": HWS, v. 2, p. 234.

183 "This is a glorious country": HWS, v. 2, p. 233.

185 "She don't believe in marriage": KHQ, v. 39, p. 522 f.n. 16.

185 "I think it is against the Bible": Maggie Harrington diary, October 8, 1867, at Douglas County Historical Museum in Lawrence, Kansas.

186 "There is not one word in the Bible": KHQ, v. 40, p. 510.

186 "carrying a squalling brat": KHQ, v. 39, p. 521.

188 "The dirt, the food!!" and "It gave me added self-respect": Griffith, Elisabeth, *In Her Own Right: The Life of Elizabeth Cady Stanton* (New York: Oxford University Press, 1984), p. 128.

There Can Be No Failure

190 Green Corn Festival: KHQ, v. 39, p. 553–554.

191 Tracks were washed out: KHQ, v. 40, p. 275.

192 "Ah, Susan,": CIHN to SBA, January 1870, quoted in KHQ, v. 40, p. 244.

192 "with sense and feeling": KHQ, v. 40, p. 276.

193 "tender love from life long acquaintance": KHQ, v. 40, p. 513.

193 "We will not hold ourselves bound": HWS, v. 2, p. 33.

194 only officials were invited: Ibid., p. 27.

194 "On every side eager hands were stretched": Ibid., p. 30.

196 "With only the right of petition": KHQ, v. 40, p. 446.

197 "depression of vitality": *Pacific Rural Press*, January 10, 1885.

197 "Dear Susan, I am very sick": KHQ, v. 40, p. 562.

Picture and Illustration Credits

Index

first lecture in Kansas 111
graduates school 18
health problems 197
helps fugitive slave 145
lectures around New England 100
lectures in 1856 campaign 136
lectures on boats 107, 116
marries first husband (Justin) 22
marries second husband (George) 39
moves to California 192
moves to Kansas Territory 106
moves to New York City 30
moves to New York State 23
moves to Quindaro 142
moves to Washington, D.C. 180
moves to Wyandotte City 186
on bloomers 76
on her appearance 20
on second-hand smoke 197
Nichols, George Bainbridge 42, 105, 115, 146, 179
Nichols, George Washington 37–40, 42, 43, 100, 104, 115, 118–120
dies 120
Nineteenth Amendment 212

P

Paine, Thomas 203
Parker, Janice 214–215
Parkville, Missouri 143, 168, 178
Paul, Alice 202, 209
Peck, James (Dimond) 168–172
Peck, Lydia 168, 170, 171
Phillips, Wendell 64, 154
Pierce, Franklin 129, 139
Pomeroy, Samuel 110
Potter Valley, California 198
Pray, Isaac C. 89
Price, Abby 62

Prohibition. *See also* temperance movement
role in passing Nineteenth Amendment 210
pro-slavery 61, 108, 126–127. *See also* Kansas

Q

Quindaro Chindowan (newspaper) 149
Quindaro, Kansas 167–172, 176, 179, 182

R

railroads 1, 60, 93, 101–102, 105, 148, 154, 192. *See also* underground railroad
Relie 121
Republican Party 135, 156, 158, 159, 166, 174, 179, 184, 188, 210
Revolutionary War 14
Robinson, Charles 132
Rose, Ernestine 87, 173, 194, 205

S

Santa Fe Trail 117
school suffrage 78–79
Seneca Falls, New York 51–52
Smith, Dr. James McCune 84
spheres 4, 21, 28, 30, 37
Stanton, Elizabeth Cady 49, 51, 53, 84, 179, 187, 188, 194, 207, 209
Stanton, Henry 49
Stone, Lucy 138, 183, 185, 206, 209
Sumner, Charles 132–133
Swisshelm, Jane 206

About the Author

Diane Eickhoff grew up on a farm in Minnesota, taught school in Appalachia and New York, and helped edit a newspaper for an anti-poverty program in Alabama. She has written widely for publications aimed at high school and younger readers. Her biography, *Revolutionary Heart*, from which this book is adapted, was named a Kansas Notable Book and the winner of *ForeWord* magazine's Book of the Year competition in biography, among other honors. She lives with her husband, author Aaron Barnhart, in Kansas City.